Never
Clean Your House
During
Hurricane
SeaSoN

Never Clean Your House During Hurricane Season

☉ Modine Gunch ☉

created by
Liz Scott
Monaghan

To Art,
whose laughter
keeps me going.
And to Katy,
the Web guru.
Thanks.

Contents

Contents

Acknowledgments

Sherry, Bob, Mike, Betsy, Bridget, Katy, Gus, Marigny, Jack, Lamont the Wonder Cat, Jack Cavalier, Dean, Abe, Theo, Ringo Starr, Joy Acosta, Tess, Mia, Mary Jane and Al LaCoste, Quinn, #4 Woolever baby, Sam, Ben, Madison, Kelly, Steven, Matt, Jen, the Chlorox bleach company, Lanie, Lesley, Shane, Vince, Mack, Tina Henderson, Anne Rice, Lynn Johnson, the makers of Shake-Away urine-based raccoon repellant, Phyllis Aleman, The Goddesses, Linda Favret, Molly's at the Market, the Window Gang, Jim, S. L. Alexander, the Saints, *New Orleans Magazine*, Morgan Packard, Faith Dawson, Julia Street, whoever manufactures Odor-Eaters, Erin Rose, Troy, Angie, Alana, Jim, the librarians of Folsom, Linda Floyd, Cathy Campbell Reichard, the late Donald E. Westlake, the present

Acknowledgments

Dave Barry, Sandra Bullock, Larry Lorenz, Brian Williams, Brad Pitt, Mark Schleifstein (who told us and told us, but would we listen?), the late Dave Dixon, The Storyville Stompers, The Loyola *Maroon* staff (past, present and future), Wolfgang Mozart, Nash Roberts, the Pulitzer-prize winning *Times-Picayune* staff, St. Jude, people of Wal-mart, and Tom and Ray Magliozzi.

Preface
by Errol Laborde

Always read Modine last. That has been my rule each month before I edit the editorial copy for the upcoming issue of *New Orleans Magazine*. I know that if I read the latest adventures of Modine Gunch before I turn to the other submitted articles, my mind will be messed up in such a way as to make my editing useless for the copy that follows. Somehow my sense of syntax is sublimated and all that I learned in school about the language is trivialized. Worst of all, and most challenging, it is difficult to edit a serious article when I am still laughing at the one before.

Modine Gunch's monthly column has developed quite a following and has even won a few awards. While Ms. Gunch is certainly an admirable woman, not enough attention is given to Liz Scott Monaghan, an accomplished writer herself, who is also Gunch's therapist, personal trainer, secretary, confessor, masseuse, spiritual advisor and yoga instructor. The two women have been together for so long that their lives have paralleled in uncanny ways, including personal relationships and Katrina experiences.

Both Gunch and Monaghan have been good for each other and have created an environment for a piece of writing that is a masterpiece. My advice to the prospective reader is this: Unless you are editing *New Orleans Magazine*, always read Modine first.

Errol Laborde is editor in chief of Renaissance Publishing. In that capacity he serves as editor/associate publisher of *New Orleans Magazine* and editor/publisher of *Louisiana Life Magazine*.

New Orleans Magazine has long been home to Modine Gunch and her domestic high jinks. But when the levees broke after Katrina, the Gunch family's houses, strung comfortably close together along one block, were among those washed away. Now the Gunches would find out that nothing that they thought was important was important after all. Yet five years later, the Gunches are still standing (when they're not second-lining.)

Never
Clean Your House
During
Hurricane
SeaSoN

Never Clean Your House During Hurricane Season

If I had known Katrina was coming, I wouldn't have spent the whole day cleaning my house.

Life is like that sometimes.

I ain't complaining. Nobody who is alive to tell the tale is complaining.

Not too much anyway.

This is what we are going to be talking about for the rest of our lives. Our great-grandchildren will beg us to please change the subject, but we won't.

We got to tell our stories. This is mine.

My mother-in-law, Ms. Larda, she followed Bob Breck's advice and had a waterproof plastic case already packed with her important papers and her kids' baby pictures. Nobody has paged through a album in her house for years, because they have been in the plastic case since Hurricane Georges missed us in 1998.

But I ran around at the last minute slinging things into cardboard boxes, and forgot half what I meant to save. I take care of my daughter Gumdrop's two cats, Rocky and Carlos, and I left with just Rocky. We didn't notice Carlos was missing until we was halfway through Mississippi. The box with my kids' baby pictures was missing too.

But I figured we'd be traipsing back in a couple of days. We had evacuated so often it was getting to be like a fire drill.

Me and my kids and most of the Gunch family had loaded in three cars before dawn that Sunday morning. My gentleman friend Lust said he would follow after he got everything tied down at the Sloth Lounge, his bar in the French Quarter.

Well, there was already so much traffic you would have thought it was Mardi Gras day. The I-10 west was bumper-to-bumper, so we got the bright idea to go east. My Aunt Chlorine in New Jersey owns this little condo in Orange Beach, Alabama. It was hit dead on by Hurricane Ivan last year, but everybody knows lighting don't strike twice in the same place, and we figured that was true for hurricanes too. So we call up Aunt Chlorine on the cell phone and she said it was almost repaired. There still ain't no elevators or phones or TV, but we were welcome there and try not to track sand on the carpet.

We get to the condo, and drag our stuff up the five flights of stairs, and then we flop down and catch our breath for a few hours, while the edge of Katrina blows over.

The next day we hike down the beach to the Flora-bama Bar to look at the news on TV. And that's how we find out what happened. We wind up camping out in front of that TV.

Lust ain't showed up, and when I call his cell phone, I get the busy signal that everybody calling New Orleans is getting.

On TV they keep saying that St. Bernard's Parish is gone. After a while we realize that they mean St. Bernard Parish. Home.

It ain't there no more.

Well. Ain't that just like God. You are sitting around worrying about will you lose weight and should you color your hair and POW—God hits you upside the head and lets you know that nothing you thought was important is important, after all.

What's important is getting your cell phone to work so you can figure out who is still alive. But I can't get hold of Lust.

Gumdrop informs me I have murdered her cat.

And then, on day three, Ms. Larda screeches and points at the TV and there is Lust being interviewed at the Sloth Lounge, which is still open because the French Quarter never flooded. And, next to him, sitting right on the bar, is Carlos.

That turns out to be the high point of my year.

All that could be salvaged from Ms. Larda's house was the crucifix over the door. At least that was meaningful. From my house, we got a sack of Mardi Gras beads—at least they was long ones—and the cat litter box.

I will fast-forward over the rest of the story. Ms. Larda is still at the condo with Leech and Lurch, and they have started a New Orleans food catering and decorated seashell business while they are waiting for a FEMA trailer. Gumdrop and her family are there too.

But the rest of us are already back in New Orleans where we belong.

My sister-in-law Gloriosa's house Uptown is OK. My other sister-in-law Larva and her family are living in Gloriosa's back yard in a camper, and they are taking turns home-schooling their kids, since there ain't no schools for them to get rid of them at.

My son Gargoyle is at LSU. My daughter Gladiola's school, Celibacy Academy, is closed for the time being, but she and a bunch of her old classmates are going to a certain Uptown school I won't mention, which had openings because a lot of their students lived in Lakeview and have moved away.

Gladiola and me have moved into the little house behind the Sloth Lounge that used to be slave quarters in the old days. Lust used to keep bar supplies there, but he cleaned it out for us. And when I walked in, there was my cardboard box with the baby pictures.

Turns out the day before Katrina hit, Lust went to my house to tell me he decided to ride out the storm at the Sloth Lounge. We had already left, but there was a box sitting in the driveway. He thought it might be important, so he took it home. And Carlos, being no fool, hopped in the truck after him.

So I got my kids and the cats and my pictures. And I can tell God I know what's important.

We all do, now.

Hosing for Christmas

The good thing about having no money is you don't have to do no Christmas shopping.

Last year, I was tearing my hair out. This Christmas, I am as relaxed as a atheist. I can actually stay home and watch *A Charlie Brown Christmas* on TV.

So Katrina did me some good.

I also discovered something I am good at. This is not the hidden talent I wish I had. If I had my choice, I would have been maybe a ballerina, or a roller derby champion.

But the talent God gave me is cleaning putrid refrigerators.

Back when I had a house, I was what you call a "casual" housekeeper, and sometimes, when things got bad, I had to take drastic measures. So, out of necessity, I developed a gag-proof refrigerator cleaning method.

Now I think maybe God is punishing me for that because I don't personally own a refrigerator no more. The last time I saw mine, it was lying on its back like a bug in Chalmette.

But for three months after Katrina, I was cleaning other people's refrigerators. I told them it was early Christmas presents. I was like the chimney sweeper in *Mary Poppins*, only I used rubber gloves and a mask and I stayed off the roof.

And I didn't sing.

I didn't even inhale.

I call my method the "Hurl and Hose Method" because it involves a lot of hurling—you can take that to mean what you want—plus, just to be safe, this little ritual I learned from my mother-in-law. (More on THAT later.)

I am thinking about patenting this method and selling it to FEMA. They ain't so good with emergencies, but maybe they can clean refrigerators for us next time.

And while I was using my method, and not breathing, I got an idea that will save the city next time.

I got to explain. I know a lot of people whose refrigerators weren't actually flooded after Katrina. They were just full of rotten food, but these people duct-taped them anyway and put them out on the curb with a message like "FEMA you" to the mayor or the governor or the president.

That don't make no sense. Send a postcard and save yourself the price of a refrigerator, I say.

The first fridge I cleaned after Katrina was behind the Sloth Lounge, in the slave quarters that Lust fixed up for me and my daughter Gladiola. He used to keep bar supplies there, and for a while a bartender lived there, but he suddenly decided to move up North.

They are a lot like that. They came to New Orleans from somewhere else and said New Orleans was their adopted home town and they would never leave. Then the levees broke and all of a sudden Minnesota looked real good.

But some of us don't know how to live anywhere else. So we got to stay, come Hell and high water.

Anyway, Lust offered to tape up this refrigerator and haul it out to the curb to save my delicate sensibilities. But I didn't have no desire to live out of a ice chest. So I took a deep breath and opened this fridge. It was stuffed with Styrofoam boxes of take-out that had given life to other things I will not mention, so I hurled and hosed and bleached and then I put in some paper plates of the same stuff I used to use when I had to air out my son Gargoyle's room: cat litter (not used), charcoal, lava rocks, and stale bread.

For the grand finale, I take a votive candle (St. Jude's is best), light it, close the door, say a rosary, and when you open it, if the candle is out, the refrigerator has been purified. That's what Ms. Larda says.

Another one was my sister-in-law Gloriosa's. She is the only one in the family who lives Uptown, and the only one whose house survived, but she been home-schooling her kids ever since the storm, so naturally she is not in her right mind. On top of which she is pregnant again.

Family is family, so I had to do something for her. Anything short of babysitting. Gloriosa is raising her children to express their selves without inhibitions and I am used to inhibiting kids upside the head when they get out of line. So I decided to clean out her refrigerator.

She couldn't open it, because she was in the throwing-up stage of pregnancy. And her husband Proteus wouldn't open it, because he is from Uptown and Uptown people don't do that. They would have just bought a new one, but Gloriosa said it was impossible to get one delivered unless you promised your firstborn son, and I was going to say that might not be a bad idea, but I came to my senses and shut my mouth.

I had forgot that they was getting ready for a sea-food party the day Katrina hit, and their meat compartment was full of crabs and oysters still in the shell. So the hurling stage was pretty bad. But right in the middle of it, maybe because of the fumes, this light bulb went off over my head and I knew how to hurricane-proof New Orleans.

We can build cement houses that snap shut like oyster shells. Or clam shells, which are smoother. Then, what we do, we don't spend our vacation money until the next Hurricane Godzilla roars in, and then we take off for a few days camping in Arizona or somewhere, and when we get back, we just open our clamshell houses and everything is dry.

We won't even need flood insurance.

Of course, the refrigerators will still smell to high heaven. But like I said, FEMA can deal with them.

They got to be good at something.

We're Still Standing

It looked like this would be the last Gunch Mardi Gras.

My sister-in-law Gloriosa wanted to make it a jazz funeral.

All because of the Christmas caroling incident.

I got to explain.

Ever since Katrina, our entire family has been living in each other's laps. My sister-in-law Larva and her husband Fred and all three of their kids are in their little vacation camper behind Gloriosa's. It is on a corner lot, so they can come and go without having to tromp through the house, at least.

Back around Christmas time, Fred was sitting there at the little pop-up table drinking his third beer. One kid was taking a shower and one was using the facilities, and Fred had to relieve himself. It was dark out because the street light right there had not worked since Katrina, so he decided to step into the yard and use the rose bush. He figured he better do it fast, so he got unzipped and ready and went out—and just then, on comes the street light and there stood a group of Christmas carolers, and they sing OoohhhhhhHHHH!!

After that, he ain't a happy camper. He says a man got to have his dignity and they are moving to Dallas.

To make it worse, the rest of us are starting to think like this. We can't live on top of each other no more. I myself got six people, a baby, two cats, and a Chihuahua in my little bitty apartment.

But my brothers-in-law Leech and Lurch are acting like nothing has changed. They are real excited because they thought of this idea to solve the carnival bathroom problem. They got one of them Pod storage containers and they are going to put it on a street near the parade route and put a potty in there, very discreet. They tell Fred all about it, as if it was only him who had this problem. This just makes Fred more upset.

(There is a flaw in the plan, because when there are a lot of Pods in a row, you don't know which Pod to pee in. We find that out later.)

But first they can't decide what we should use for costumes, blue tarps or refrigerator cartons. Most of the Gunches are on the hefty side, so either one would be a good fit. The boys collect a few cartons and paint them like refrigerators and put duct tape around them. They even write "Thanks, FEMA" on them.

Fred sees them collected in the yard and says if these are supposed to be our new homes, he ain't surprised. And he storms off to get a road map of Texas.

Things are not good here. My friend Awlette, who I have gone out with every Mardi Gras since high school, calls me from Chicago and says she is personally insulted that they are having Mardi Gras without her. And cousin Luna is in Phoenix, and Lysolla who used to live next door is in Sault Ste. Marie, Michigan. How can they have Mardi Gras when everybody can't come?

Gloriosa starts pushing her jazz funeral idea. She says we can use black trash bags for shrouds and make the refrigerator cartons into coffins. And we could get my cousin Snapfoot and his band to march in front and play "Do You Know What It Means To Miss New Orleans?" and sad dirges like that.

We are sitting knee-to-knee—which is the only way we can sit in my apartment—with my mother-in-law Ms. Larda.

"Laissez les bon temps finito!" Gloriosa says, a little too loud, because the baby wakes up.

Ms. Larda shakes her head. She says, "Listen, if I was battling a fatal disease, would I run around in a shroud to show I am sad about it? That don't make no sense."

Glorisoa says we will be sending a message—a distress call with the whole world watching.

"Sometimes you just got to fix things yourself, Gloriosa," Ms. Larda says.

I carry the baby outside then, so I don't hear no more of what Ms. Larda is saying, but I wonder if she is thinking about fixing up the refrigerator cartons and moving in.

When I come back, she is on her cell phone. She stays on the phone for the next two days. She pulls a sweatband over her ears, and she got the phone stuck in there and every once in a while she yanks it out and punches some numbers, and sticks it back in. She talks and she listens and sometimes she reads her book of St. Jude novena prayers, so I know she got the big guns out. She read them prayers the whole time we was evacuating.

Finally she pulls the phone off her ear and clears her throat and we all—there are six of us in the room at the time—look at her. She announces that there are two FEMA trailers being set up right that minute where her house used to be—one for her and one for Leech and Lurch.

And while we are cheering and clutching each other over that, Larva calls and says she and Fred have just rented a house in Metairie, of all places. It had a little Broussard water in it, but that's all cleaned up and it's got new carpets and the owner is keeping the rent low because he owes a favor to St. Jude for saving his own mama from the flood.

A coincidence?

We are still going to use cousin Snapfoot and the band. Come Mardi Gras day, they will launch into "I'm Still Standing" and off we will strut in capes made out of blue tarps.

And if Ms. Larda can work it with St. Jude and the politicians, we'll be strutting next year too.

Let 'em roll.

How to Pass a Good Time

Nobody can say my little sister-in-law Gloriosa ain't a good mother.

She knows that there are a lot of evils in this world, and her kids ain't going to enjoy any of them.

I got to explain. My mother-in-law, Ms. Larda, had five children, and Gloriosa, besides being the family beauty, was the one born after the sexual revolution.

The rest of her kids was brought up like me. Sin was on the top of our list of evils.

But Gloriosa never worried about sin. From the time she grew bosoms, she kept Ms. Larda busy making back-to-back novenas to keep her from going to Hell or getting a tattoo. Gloriosa was definitely a free spirit.

Things have changed.

Gloriosa is a Mommy.

Now she got a whole list of evils—but they are new evils, like breathing in a room where a cigarette has been smoked, eating sugared cereal, drinking Coke, or watching a TV show where sex is mentioned.

She is also convinced that most of New Orleans is now a bubbling toxic soup, so her kids are not allowed to inhale unless they are Uptown. Even though Ms. Larda is their mawmaw, she is in a trailer in Chalmette, so Gloriosa won't let them go see her.

Ms. Larda acts like this is tragic, but she is really pretty happy about it. Them kids are being brought up to express their little selves, and there ain't much room for expressing in a two-room trailer.

Besides, Gloriosa has informed us all that her kids do not refer to their body parts by any old-fashioned euphemisms like whosis or peepee. They use anatomically correct names that make Ms. Larda's hair stand up on end. She would have got her mouth washed out with soap for saying those words out loud.

Besides all this, Gloriosa has married into Uptownery—natural beauty and large bosoms can take a girl a long way. Now she got social connections that the Gunches don't blend in with.

Her little boy Comus was about to become four years old. This was a major event. She planned a birthday gala and invited the important people that her husband Proteus does business with; plus Proteus's family; plus a few token guests that are actually children, and last but not least, the Gunch connection. I think this has her worried. Most of the family lives in trailers now, and you know how the upper crust feels about trailer people.

Gloriosa told Ms. Larda to remind everybody to shower before they leave Chalmette, and that the men should wear ties. Ms. Larda says she will also remind them to wear pants. But Gloriosa don't laugh. She just frowns, like she should of mentioned that herself.

But the Saturday before the party, she stops by my apartment for a secret Diet Coke fix—this is her new vice—and says she needs a favor. Some of her husband's uncles like their cigars, and Gloriosa wants to tell them, in a classy way, not to light up in the house. My daughter Gladiola is the artsy type, and Gloriosa wants her to paint a sign that says "no smoke," in three different languages, like the signs in Europe. I seen signs like that in people's driveways in the French Quarter. They read "stationnement interdit," which means "no parking" in French.

I say nobody can read them signs, but she says MOST of the people who are coming to this party speak multiple languages.

Then she tells me a long story about how she and Proteus honeymooned in Europe and she was sitting in the john on a train looking at a sign written in eight languages and didn't realize until she got to the last translation in English that it said "Do not relieve yourself while the train is in the station," and she had already broken that rule.

But she is bringing up her kids to know better. They listen to French and Spanish nursery rhyme CDs when they drive around town in the Beamer, wearing little surgical masks so they won't inhale no toxic mold.

Anyway, I tell Gladiola and my son Gargoyle about the dress code for this birthday party. I wait patiently until Gargoyle gets done making barf noises about the tie, and then I ask Gladiola to paint the sign. Gargoyle brightens right up and says he will look up the translations on his new computer. Gladiola rescues a sign that used to be on the neutral ground saying a nail salon was now open, and she paints over that and draws little smiley and frowny faces on puffs of smoke. Then she copies the translation Gargoyle wrote out, "No peter. No pedo. No smoke," in balloon letters.

It turns out to be a very genteel party. Everybody walks around being genteel all over the place. And they all look at Gladiola's little sign, and they tell her how precious it is. There is a Mexican lady named Lupe serving refreshments. I notice she keeps breaking out into giggles.

I decide to leave after the string quartet finishes "Happy Birthday." As I am going out the door, Lupe runs after me with my souvenir slice of birthday cake in a little box with Comus's picture on it. She is giggling again, and I got to ask what's so funny, and she points to the sign. I say, "'No smoke' is funny?" and then she whispers what the sign really says.

Well. I rush home to Gargoyle's computer and look it up. And it's true.

That sign does not say "No smoke" in Spanish. It says, like Lupe put it, no . . . what people do when they ate too many beans.

I think about that. All them Uptown people saying how precious that sign was. I guess them people don't speak multiple languages after all.

Or they didn't listen to the right nursery rhymes.

I'm Cool

This planet hit menopause at the same time I did.

It has global warming; I have hot flashes.

Now this got nothing to do with the kind of flashing certain types of people do for beads.

This is the kind of flashing where you heat up from the inside like somebody turned your thermostat up, and then a few minutes later, you are freezing.

They could have used me for a traffic light a few months ago when we didn't have nothing but four-way stops in this city.

I called up my friend Awlette and told her about it, but she just said she wishes she had some of them hot flashes herself. She is still freezing her unmentionables off in Chicago, and here it is April.

Then she tells me I should try soy in my diet. I tell her, I eat Chinese food at least once a week and I use two or three packets of the soy sauce that come with it every single time, but I still got hot flashes.

A while back I happen to be in the Walgreens, and lo and behold, they are selling "hot flash cool-down strips." The sign says they were invented by a leading gynecologist and will work discreetly for hours. I pay $10 of my good FEMA money for a box of five, and I put them in my purse and I go off to meet my gentle-man friend Lust for lunch at Stanley's over there on Decatur Street.

I feel a hot flash coming on even before we order, so I take the package out behind the menu, and I read the directions, and it says to slap one on the back of your neck. Well. That ain't discreet. I excuse myself and go to the Ladies, still flashing, and I open the pack and each strip is encased in a little plastic pouch, which it turns out you can't open without a weapon. I slash at it with my car keys, and I chew at it a while, and finally my hot flash goes away on its own, so I go back to the table. At least I saved myself $2.

I bet that leading gynecologist was a man. And what is he doing telling me to put something on my neck? The neck ain't hardly his area of expertise.

One day I am standing in front the refrigerator fanning the door back and forth to cool off. I am also checking on what's to eat, and I notice a head of cabbage that's been in there. Ms. Larda caught it at the

St. Patrick's Day parade. Usually she takes them home and cooks them up, but her trailer is pretty small and she don't like to eat cabbage when she is in small quarters, if you know what I mean.

And while I am looking at it, a light bulb pops on over my head.

About a month before Katrina, I remember I read this weird story in the papers about a South Korean baseball pitcher named Park Myung-Hwan, who used to get real hot when he was playing baseball out in the sun. He didn't have no gel strips, but what he did, he froze cabbage leaves and put them under his hat. Only one day his hat fell off and the South Korean baseball officials were shocked to see cabbage leaves on this man's head. I guess cabbage leaves on the head signifies something really nasty in Korea. Anyway, they made him stop.

Well, I don't have no Korean baseball officials to answer to, so this seems like a good idea. Except I don't wear a hat. And if I slapped a cabbage leaf on the back of my neck, it wouldn't be discreet.

Then I think of just where to put them.

First, I freeze all the individual leaves on a cookie sheet in my freezer.

Next hot flash, I take two leaves and shove them in my bra. And aaaahhhh—no more hot flash. Just like that. I have discovered the cure,

I can sell them and get rich. I will call them "organic bosom coolers."

Of course, there is one disadvantage to these coolers—they present problems when I am in public.

I find this out when Lust takes me out to dinner. I put on a pair of cabbage leaves before I leave. I also pack a spare pair in a plastic bag with two of them blue cold compresses (the kind you keep in the freezer for when somebody bumps their head) and then I stuff them in my purse. I barely manage to snap it closed, but I am ready for flashes.

Lust even compliments me on my figure. He says I look particularly buxom. I tell him it's all in his mind. He says it's always on his mind. Ain't that the truth.

Lust is in the mood for Chinese, and we wind up going all the way to Metairie to a Oriental buffet. We are on our second platefuls when I start to heat up, so I excuse myself to head for the Ladies to put in a fresh pair of bosom coolers, but when I pick up my purse, it pops open, and my whole refrigerator pack spills out on the floor.

The waiter looks down at it and says, "Planning to take home a few extra shrimp?"

I got no idea what he is talking about, but come to find out they have been having problems with people stuffing their faces and then scooping a couple more meals into their purses. And these people have purses equipped like mine.

So he calls the manager over. And then, right in front of everybody, I got to explain about the hot flashes and the bosom coolers and Park Myung-

Hwan. I even show them the cabbage leaves. Thank God frozen raw cabbage leaves aren't on the menu. Besides, I guess they decide nobody would make up a story like that.

So they apologize. And to make up, they give me a whole box of soy sauce packets.

I hope this planet does better with the global warming.

When the Trailer's Rockin' . . .

The Gunches are double-wide and their FEMA trailers ain't.

That is getting to be a problem.

Thank goodness my mother-in-law Ms. Larda got one all to herself, but even so, she says the shower is a tight fit. She can't get to all her necessary parts without bending over, and there ain't no room to bend over, so she got to soap up first, then go in and try to rinse off. She says she would be qualified to be a Yogi before this is over, if it wasn't against her religion.

Ms. Larda is very dependent on her religion right now, because she got St. Jude to thank for her FEMA trailer. She didn't get nothing from FEMA until she done her flying novena to St. Jude.

In case you don't know, a regular novena is nine days of praying—not just any prayers but special never-known-to-fail prayers. But if you don't got nine days, you can do a flying novena, which means you stuff all the prayers into maybe nine hours, which Ms. Larda did while she was on hold with the government people.

She must have been a prayer or two short though, because she got the trailer but no electricity. The FEMA people said to call Entergy and the Entergy people said to call FEMA. So she called up Channel 6 and that worked. When heaven lets you down, go to the Action Reporter.

But now she's been in the trailer three months, with one more month until hurricane season, and she is getting stressed out.

She practically jumps out her skin when I knock on the door.

"I thought you was somebody with more bad news, Modine," she says to me.

The latest bad news is that my daughter Gumdrop and her husband and my only grandbaby, born a year ago on Carnival Day in the middle of the parade, are leaving New Orleans.

This hit us all pretty hard, and it pushed Ms. Larda over the edge. We are used to her being as solid as the rocket of Gibraltar, so we got to do something.

Me and my sister-in-law Larva was at Lakeside Shopping Center, trying to find something that might cheer her up for Mother's Day and we pass one of them stores that sells all them technological gizmos that you never knew you couldn't live without. And there, in the front, is this woman testing out a electronic reclining chair. She looks so relaxed I think she is dead. But she ain't. She is bobbing very gently, like she is floating on a rubber raft in a motel pool and there ain't nobody else there. This chair is massaging every part of her—her legs, her arms, her buns, her back, even her neck. It is a beautiful thing to see.

It is the perfect gift. If this don't de-stress Ms. Larda, we are going to have to look for hard drugs.

It takes a lot of doing, but me and all the Gunches and even my gentleman friend Lust chip in and we put together enough for this recliner.

We get it delivered ahead of time, so she will have a few days of relaxing before we all get together on Mother's Day.

We hope she is relaxed enough to cook. The Gunches usually celebrate holidays by eating, but we ain't put on a good feed bag since before Katrina. For Easter, we sent out for pizza. That ain't right.

Of course, what none of us realizes is if you can't fit a decent shower in this trailer, how are you going to fit in a recliner that moves? That's what the men said when they showed up to set it up.

But like I said, when Ms. Larda makes up her

mind, don't argue. So they wedged it in, even though there is no room whatsoever left in the trailer.

When I go by there the next day, even before I get to the steps, I notice this trailer is shaking.

It reminds me of that saying, "When this trailer is a-rockin', don't come a-knockin'." But I push open the door—and there is Ms. Larda laid out in this chair, facing away from me, with her head back and her mouth hung open. Her bosoms are all a-jiggle and her stomach is bobbing like a beach ball on the open sea. The rest of the trailer is also in motion. The plates in her cabinet are clinking and the coffee cups are swinging on their hooks and her coffee pot is tap dancing. Forget hurricanes—we got an earthquake going right here in this trailer.

I try to tap her shoulder, but that is rippling too. Finally I reach around and push the power button and everything quivers to a stop.

Ms. Larda opens her eyes and looks up at me. "I been like this all day," she says. "I can't get to the front door, but I don't care."

So we all got to chip in again and rent one of them storage pods and set it up next to the trailer. Then we manage to take the chair apart and put it in the pod, and run an extension cord out there to give it power. Of course, the front door of this pod raises up like a garage door, so if Ms. Larda wants to catch some breeze, she got to shiver and shake in front of the entire parish—not that there's much left of that. She could charge admission, but what she does is let people buy a few minutes in the chair—real cheap—so they can get unstressed too.

Maybe we should rent another pod and set up a shower. Double-wide.

Oysters and Oreos

She can't fit in her shower no more, so my mother-in-law decides to go on a diet.

Now, I got to explain. It ain't a normal shower she can't fit in. It is a FEMA trailer shower, which is understandable. Half the people in Chalmette can't fit into their FEMA showers. That's why they got all them hoses rigged up on poles next to the trailers.

Because of modesty purposes, most people only shower at night. Which is why you should never drive around the Parish after 9 P.M. with night goggles on, unless you are a pervert.

But Ms. Larda worries about this, so she asks if she can shower at my apartment, which is in back of my gentleman friend Lust's Sloth Lounge in the Quarter. And while she is in there with her clothes off, she wants me to run down to the Quarter Launderette and run a couple loads of laundry for her, being as she don't have a washer in her trailer.

When I get back, she is sitting on a barstool in the Lounge in her hot pink terrycloth robe telling Lloyd the bartender about how her trailer is so small she can stir her beans while she is on the toilet. He feels sorry for her and treats her to a frozen Irish coffee, which is not on any diet.

Next thing, my sister-in-law Larva waltzes in. She got weight problems too, which she proceeds to tell us about over a cranberry-and-vodka. She says she had enough time to get pregnant and have a entire baby since Katrina, and she should have done it because she gained just as much weight but she ain't got no baby to show for it.

It ain't just them. Before Katrina, I myself was never fat, but before Katrina I never sucked down a entire bag of Oreos during one episode of *American Idol*. Tight clothes are in style, but I am so stylish I can't tie my shoes with my blue jeans on.

What is it about hurricanes that make you hungry? Maybe this is God's way—fatten us up, so if we get another flood we can float out of here without no life jackets.

But if there's another flood, we ain't hanging around, so we might as well get rid of this fat.

Ms. Larda used to swear by Sugar Busters, but her diet book washed away with her kitchen, which is the one good thing to come out of this, being as she used to carry slabs of bacon in her purse for snacks.

Larva says she would like to try Weight Watchers, but it costs good money, which we don't have a lot of these days. Then I come up with one of my brilliant ideas. We will all chip in for her to join, and she can go to the meetings and then tell the rest of us what they said, so we can all follow the plan for the price of one.

She goes the very next day, and when she comes back, she tells us that they don't count calories and they don't count carbs, they count points. You get a certain number of points a day to eat, depending on how fat you are to start with. I, for instance, can eat 20 points worth a day.

Every food is worth a different number of points. Broccoli and celery and stuff like that got no points, so you can eat as much as you want, not that you want much. But every Oreo cookie counts for one-and-a-third points. So if I eat a 16-cookie bag, and don't eat nothing whatsoever else all day, I still have eaten more than my 20 points.

I hide my Oreos in the freezer, for when I am skinny again, and for a entire week, I carry a calculator around trying to figure out what I can eat next.

Then Larva goes to her second meeting and comes over with big news. She has lost two pounds, and better yet, she has found out raw oysters got no points. They are as good as celery. But they got to be raw.

Now, I never thought I would be slurping down

raw oysters in a month that don't have an R in it, but that don't matter now. My brothers-in-law Leech and Lurch got a friend who comes up with a couple sacks of them, and we all sit out in front of Ms. Larda's trailer and eat them as fast as we can shuck them.

That night when I am going to bed, I stop in front of the freezer. I realize that, thanks to them oysters, I haven't used up hardly any of my points today. So just to keep things even, I should eat a couple Oreos.

I eat the whole bag. Still frozen.

Well. I still don't know if I got a bad oyster or you just shouldn't wash down oysters with frozen Oreos. I do know I ain't going to eat either of them ever again.

I spent the next 24 hours in my bathroom, and I ain't going to say anything else about that because I don't want to think about it.

But my clothes ain't tight no more.

I called up Ms. Larda to ask if she got sick and she said she didn't and neither did Larva. But they have had a talk and decided God wants them to stop cheating Weight Watchers. So they will both find the money to pay and they will go to the meetings together, and they will stick with it until they are back at their pre-Katrina weight.

She should fit back into her shower any time now, she says.

Too bad for them perverts.

Way Up Yonder

All her life, my daughter Gumdrop has lived in a normal house where the mail dropped through a slot in the door.

Not no more. Now her mailbox will set out by the road, and have one of them little red flags on it. Gumdrop is moving to the country.

This ain't good news, being as she is taking along my grandbaby, Lollipop.

But it ain't entirely bad, being as she is also taking along her husband, Slime.

The poor things couldn't find nowhere to live in the Parish, or in New Orleans, or even out in Jefferson, and they never got no FEMA trailer. They been camping out with this one and that one, and finally when Slime's parents Dr. and Dr. Slime (they are both dentists) offered them free rent on a log cabin in Folsom, way up on the Northshore, they took them up on it.

The senior Slimes were getting ready to retire there, out with the birds and the bees and the chickadees and such, which is evidently what they like after spending most of their lives with their hands down people's throats.

I myself like a little human noise now and again, but I guess the Slimes have heard enough of that. Anyway, they had financial reverses because of Katrina, and they are going to put it off a few years.

So meanwhile, Gumdrop is going to live in their log cabin with her little family. Now this is a girl who always lived in a house where, even with the windows closed and the air conditioner going full blast, you could hear the neighborly sounds like somebody beating out the dents in a fender, or testing the speakers in their pickup, and where the McDonald's was only five minutes away.

This is going to be a culture shock.

I try to warn her. I tell her everything I know about country life, which I have heard straight from the horse's mouth of my cousin Luna from Denham Springs. They don't got front lawns and back yards in the country. They got acres. Now, in the city, an acre would be enough for a couple houses and a gas station, but in the country, they just let their acres sit around the house and grow trees, or they raise animals on them. And I am not talking normal animals, like cats and dogs and gerbils and them. I am talking horses. Cows. God knows what.

And in the country people don't say "How ya' doin'?" when they see each other because they ain't close enough to talk. People in the country spend a lot of time Yonder, wherever that is, so when they see someone Yonder, they wave. Cousin Luna is near-sighted, so she has been known to wave at her own mailbox, but she says a lot people do that.

Gumdrop will have plenty to get used to. But first things first. We got to get her there.

Moving wasn't no problem for most people in our family after Katrina, being as we didn't have nothing left to move. We just walked right in our new apartment or our FEMA trailer and put our purse on the table and that was it.

Every disaster has a silver lining.

Gumdrop and Slime are an exception, because they have actual furniture. They was just in the process of moving back to New Orleans before Katrina and most of their furniture was still in storage out in the part of Metairie that didn't get no flood water.

They got an armoire, a china cabinet, a fake leather couch, and a side-by-side Frigidaire and freezer. And that ain't all. Slime—who probably weighs 130 pounds full of beer—secretly desires to be Arnold Schwarzenegger, and he got this weight-lifting contraption which stands nine feet high and has a lot of cords and weights and pulleys on it. Anybody who lifts that thing got no more use for exercise equipment. They either got the strength of Goliath or they are dead.

So their move is going to be complicated.

They decide to rent a U-Haul, and on moving day, we send my brothers-in-law Lurch and Leech to the Home Depot to hire a couple of immigrant workers to help with the heavy lifting.

The rest of us meet at the storage place, and wait for Leech and Lurch to show up with the immigrants.

We wait, and then we wait some more. Finally my mother-in-law Ms. Larda notices two gentlemen working on a roof across the street. She goes over and stands at the bottom of their ladder until one of them comes down, and then she speaks very loud, since she assumes he don't understand English. Turns out he does understand English, but he assumes she is deaf as a post, being as she is yelling, so he answers her very loud, so all of us and everybody else in two blocks hear a play-by-play of the negotiating.

Anyway, they settle on $50, and the two of them, Diego and Pancho, come across the street and help Slime load the U-Haul. They are just finishing when Lurch and Leech come staggering up. They said they was standing in front the Home Depot looking for immigrants and some guy came up and offered them $50 to help move a grand piano, so they went off and did that. Now they are too tired to do anything else.

Well. Ms. Larda don't have to speak loud to them. She don't have to speak at all. She looks at them, and they look at her, and she puts out her hand and they hand over the $50, and she passes it to Diego and Pancho, who say THANK YOU very loud.

Then Gumdrop and Slime and the baby drive off to their new life way up Yonder, not in New Orleans.

Temporary Relief

My mother-in-law, Ms. Larda, says all this hurricane stress has given her nerves and prostration, and worse. She also got gastronomical problems.

"Hurricanes can cause more than one kind of wind, if you know what I mean," she says to me, out the side of her mouth.

She has had this problem before, and she cured it with Beano and a candle to St. Jude, but neither one is coming through for her this time.

She says she wouldn't worry about it usually, and just let it pass, so to speak, but this FEMA trailer she is living in is too small for that. "Somebody strikes a match in here and the whole thing will blow up, Modine," she says to me. She saw a story about that on TV one time, but it was cows in a barn in England, and they barely got out with their lives.

So she carried her statue of St. Jude outside before she lit the candle in front of it.

She knows she needs to go to the doctor, but her doctor ain't there no more. All his patients are supposed to go to this other doctor out in Metairie, who is so busy even his nurse got voice mail. You leave a message with your name, date of birth, health insurance company, and what symptoms you are experiencing, and she will supposedly get back to you one of these days.

Ms. Larda answers the first three questions. Then she gets to the part about describing her symptoms. She don't know how to do that in a ladylike way. So she hangs up.

God knows what the nurse would have done with that voice mail. Maybe she would secretly play it to all the other nurses on their lunch break and they would have a good laugh. Maybe they would send it in to "World's Funniest Videos—the Voice Mail Version" and she would get her 15 minutes of fame for flatulence.

She calls this nurse back and says she got chest pains, because she figures a actual human being will call her back for that, and she can explain.

Meanwhile, my daughter Gumdrop is calling me, but her cell phone don't work where she is and I only hear every other word she is saying: "Mama . . . in-law . . . RACCOON . . . too far . . . come."

She and her husband Slime and my little grand-baby have moved to the country, up in Folsom.

Well, I intend to evacuate to her house when the time comes anyway, and I might as well check the place out, so me and my gentleman friend Lust and my littlest daughter Gladiola, we cross the Causeway and keep going, past all these acres which have grass and horses and split-rail fences like in western movies, down a long road and up a hill to the log cabin where Gumdrop is. I am astounded. A hill. Gumdrop was never on no hill except Monkey Hill in Audubon Park in her whole life, and here she is on a hill.

She comes running out and flings her arms around us like she hasn't seen us for a year instead of a week ago when she moved, and she shows us around the house, which is pretty nice, because it ain't really made out of real logs; it just gives that effect. It belongs to Slime's parents, but Gumdrop and Slime are living in it for now because they can't find noplace else.

Then she brings us out to the back acre—this is what they call back yards in the country—and there is a little small log cabin that matches the big one. I ask if this is for the goats or what, and she says this is the mother-in-law house, and lots of people build them these days. Then she drops the bomb. She asks would I come live there for a while and look after the baby while she goes back to work. She says Gladiola could even go to St. Scholastica Academy, which is around there somewhere.

Gladiola reacts to this like she stepped in pig doodoo, so I know she don't like that idea. And me, I got Lust. I got a life. Gumdrop says to think about it. I think no, but I don't say so.

When we get back home, Ms. Larda is on the phone saying the nurse called back about the chest pains. Ms. Larda was ready for her. She says she solved that by getting a bigger bra, but now she got her on the phone, she wants to talk about a more delicate problem. And she does. So they run a bunch of tests, which Ms. Larda don't want to talk about.

After a week, the nurse calls and says Ms. Larda ain't going to die from this problem—which is good, because how would that look on her tombstone, Ms. Larda says. But she is supposed to take some pink pills and avoid stress.

"So how do I sit in a FEMA trailer during hurricane season and avoid stress?" she says to me. She lit another candle in front of St. Jude, but she don't know how much good that will do, even is he is the Saint of the Impossible.

I have a stroke of genius. "How about a nice little cabin on a hill?" I say.

"Hill? Like Monkey Hill?" says Ms. Larda.

So I explain, and the next week we truck Ms. Larda and her statue and her massage recliner over the Causeway and through the woods to Gumdrop's place, which we now call Monkey Hill North.

I don't know how long she is going to last up there.

You can only stand so much peace and quiet. But she says she'll hang in until hurricane season is over.

Meanwhile, her gastronomical problem has evaporated into thin air.

You can always count on St. Jude.

Halloween
of Hope

New Orleans is hanging on by its fingernails.

But my friend Awlette is here to fix it.

She is opening a manicure salon.

She says there is no place on earth where as many fingernails are suffering as right here, with people using them to scrape off mold and pry out screws and peel wet pictures apart and God knows what else.

She has been staying in Chicago, but she says she'd rather drown here than freeze there, so she went out and got a business loan and a garage apartment Uptown, and here she is.

And then she offers me a job.

Which is a good thing, being as I have reorganized my gentleman friend Lust's office above the Sloth Lounge so good he can't find anything. He been dropping hints that I could maybe find another job somewhere else. Business and romance don't mix, he says to me, only he don't say it as poetic as that. Don't spit where you eat, is what he says. Or something like that.

Of course, to take this new job, Awlette says I got to go to beauty school, plus do 100 sets of toes and 100 sets of fingers before I am allowed to do anybody's fingers and toes for money.

I ain't been to school since I graduated from high school at Celibacy Academy, so I don't know. Maybe I have gotten stupider over the years and ain't in a fit state to learn anything. I am thinking about this when my little daughter Gladiola storms in from her new high school and announces that she has to be the jack o' lantern effect.

Now, if you been living here, you know the jack o' lantern effect is what they call it if just one or two people come back and turn on their lights in a neighborhood that was demolished by the hurricane—and all around them are houses that are dark and empty.

So how can she be the jack o' lantern effect? Then she explains. She is talking about the Halloween dance at her new school. She thought of the theme "Jack o' Lantern Effect" and her friend Mawlene thought of "Ghosts that Ain't There No More" and they are each going to school in a costume that will illustrate the theme, and then the whole class will vote.

Mawlene will wear a sheet and a sign around her

neck that reads D.H. Holmes's, Kirschman's, Krause's, K & B, Rocky and Carlo's, Camellia Grill—places that ain't there no more, like in Benny Grunch's song. But she is going to be a sexy ghost, and her sheet will probably be a pillowcase, Gladiola says.

Now if they were still going to Celibacy Academy, she would be swathed in a king-size sheet. Sister Gargantua would see to that. But Celibacy Academy ain't there no more.

So Gladiola needs a jack o' lantern effect costume. And it needs to be gorgeous.

Costume making in our family is usually a job for my mother-in-law, Ms. Larda, but she is in Folsom with my older daughter Gumdrop, helping out with Gumdrop's little girl, especially now that Gumdrop has morning sickness because of her baby bump. (That is what they say instead of "bun in the oven" these days.)

Whenever Ms. Larda can't make a costume, I whip one up out of plastic garbage bags and duct tape. But Gladiola refuses to go to her new school wearing a garbage bag. She says she got a better idea. She will paint herself orange and put black triangular eyes on each boob and a black triangle nose on her navel and a black smile on her . . . I stop her right there.

We got to get Celibacy Academy up and running again.

I promise to think of something glamorous that don't involve garbage bags. Then I call Awlette.

Gladiola wants glamor, I tell her. But jack o' lanterns are orange and round, and glamor is skinny with large bosoms.

Awlette says, "She isn't going to be a jack o'lantern. She is going to be an effect."

So how does an effect dress? We decide we need inspiration, so that night we drive to our old neighborhood in Chalmette. There, on my block, I see one house and one FEMA trailer with lights in the window. Everything else is black as velvet.

We drive home without much to say.

But the wheels are churning in Awlette's head.

Everything should be black, except for a couple of lights, she says.

Next day she turns up with a bolt of black velvet, a sheer black scarf, and a sheet of poster paper and whips them into a princess hat. Then we get some of them flashing pendants with the tiny little chip batteries, and make triangle eyes and a nose and a mouth that light up. These we put on the hat.

Next day we go out to Lakeside Mall and I get her a slinky little black dress. It is low enough in front to show a little cleavage, if she had cleavage, which she don't, so I don't feel like I have to explain myself to Sister Gargantua.

So she waltzes off to school in that—all black except for a few lights, and Mawlene is there in her pillowcase—a stretch knit one that is practically form-fitting, Gladiola tells me later.

And would you believe, it is a tie. So the student council decides they will just combine the themes and call the dance "The Jack o' Lantern Effect Ain't There No More: Halloween of Hope."

All that positive thinking is contagious, so I take a deep breath and I sign up for beauty school.

Awlette and me, we will rebuild New Orleans, one fingernail at a time.

How to Outwit a Smart-Aleck Bear

Maybe it is just the Zoloft talking, but my friend Awlette claims you can find something good about anything, even hurricane evacuations.

For instance, she says, after Katrina we all learned new technological skills—like how to text message on our cell phones.

Now, before Katrina, the only people who knew how to use text messaging were kids cheating on their tests in school. But right after Katrina, everybody from New Orleans figured it out, because that was the only way you could get ahold of anybody.

Well, whoop-de-doo, I say.

You have to tap three times for every single letter in a text message, so you abbreviate every word, and by the time you do this, and the person who gets it figures out what "Wht X R U gng 2 chrch Sndy?" means, it is probably already Sndy and you have missed chrch.

Smoke signals would work better.

My oldest daughter Gumdrop is living up in Folsom with her husband Slime, and now my mother-in-law Ms. Larda is up there with them, taking care of their baby while Gumdrop goes to work.

They got no house phone and the cell phones they bought on sale keep losing their signals. But just like after Katrina, they can text message.

Last week me and my gentleman friend Lust was waiting for the pizza man, and I hear the doorbell chime, and I rush to the door but there ain't nobody there. It is my cell phone. This is its cutesy way of telling me I got a text message.

It is from Ms. Larda. "Tlkng bear drvng me nts," it says.

Tlkng bear?

Now, Ms. Larda has what you might call "a way with words." A strange way. Like for instance, last time we evacuated, we passed the sign that says Causeway on the bridge leading to the North Shore, and she says, "Why do they spell it like that? They should spell it like it sounds."

I got to think about that. Naturally, she talks like everybody else from New Orleans, and when we say "car," we pronounce it "caw." Come to find out, she thinks this bridge is called the "caws-way" because the caws go that way.

And now she is sending me messages about a tlking bear. God know what that means.

The phone chimes again, and I think it is the pizza man again, but it is Gumdrop.

Between work and being a mama, Gumdrop is always in a rush, so she abbreviates even more than most people do. This means I never have a clue what she is saying. All I know is she is alive, or else she was alive a few minutes ago and her last dying wish was to send me a string of consonants.

This message says, "Xpctng! Fts 37 cells."

I show it to Lust.

He says, "Cells? Slime in jail?"

"For what?" I say.

"They got strange laws out in the country. Maybe he expectorated on the sidewalk."

I start pecking out "Slm n jl?" on my phone, and then I hear a real loud chime, which turns out to be the pizza man. I drop the phone, and would you believe, it lands in my soothing lavender aromatherapy fountain. This turns out to be just as bad as dropping it in the toilet, which I have also done. So now I learned something else about technology. Water ain't good for it.

But I got to find out what on earth is going on in Folsom. So on Sunday morning, I visit the ATM, fill up the gas tank, and drive out there.

I pull up in front the cabin, and there is Slime, flopped in a hammock on the porch. Lollipop, the baby, is in his lap holding her Winnie-the-Pooh bear.

Gumdrop rushes out all excited and asks what I thought about her message, and without stopping for me to answer, bursts out, "Slime and I are expecting another baby!"

Then she explains that they have calculated that their fetus is already 37 cells big. That's what she meant by cells. Gumdrop is the scientific type.

That's what the message said. Slime never expectorated at all. Or if he did, he didn't get caught.

So I give her a hug and Lollipop a hug and even hug Slime.

I am about to ask about Ms. Larda when a shrill little voice says, "It's time for me to have a healthy snack."

I look at Lollipop, but she can't talk yet. It's the bear. Gumdrop tells me this is a talking Winnie-the-Pooh with a digital voice box inside, and you can program it to say whatever you want, whenever you want.

And she got the brilliant idea to program the Lollipop's daily schedule into this bear. It reminds you, in its high-pitched voice, when it is snack time, bath time, meal time, and nap time. That way Ms. Larda will always know what to do.

So Ms. Larda, who raised five kids and helped raise a horde of grandchildren, is being ordered around by Winnie-the-Pooh.

That's what that text message was about.

I pick up this wondrous bear and go around back and find Ms. Larda sipping on a cup of coffee the size of a cereal bowl. I just know she got a shot of Kahlua in there. She says she is glad I drove up, because she was thinking of making like Fats Domino and walking to New Orleans.

I tell her this bear is a technological problem and I am a expert on technology now. I unzip Winnie's back, take out his voicebox, drop it into the coffee mug, fish it out with a spoon, wipe it off on my shirt, and put it back inside him.

He won't bother Ms. Larda no more.

Awlette is going to be proud.

A New Tradition

Used to be, everybody in the Gunch family was omnivorous. They ate anything and the more the better.

But now we got picky eaters.

My sister-in-law Gloriosa, who has transformed from a free spirit with large boobs into a Uptown matron with kids, rules out red meat for health reasons. Also, she sends her kids to nursery at the Jewish Community Center and some of the other children there were not allowed to eat shellfish and she figured they must know something we don't know, so she ruled that out too.

My other sister-in-law, Larva, is the last surviving Sugar Buster dieter in this city. But she goes Sugar

Busters one better. She won't eat nothing that isn't meat. Except maybe some Crisco out of the can.

My daughter Gumdrop is pregnant again, so she got a long list of things she ain't allowed to have: sprouts, tuna fish, sweeteners, coffee, alcohol of any kind, blah, blah, blah. I ate all those things and none of my kids came out too weird, but now the experts say one wrong bite and God knows what could happen to your baby. So Gumdrop is swearing off all of them, not to mention food in general, being as she is at the throwing-up stage of expectancy.

She also informs me that my granddaughter Lollipop only eats things that she can pick up off her high chair tray with her tiny fingers, plus strained fruits and vegetables that are spooned down her little gullet while you are making airplane noises. No onions or garlic. Now I have seen this child scarf down a African violet right off the window sill in 15 seconds, but I am not going to mention that.

Naturally, this presents a problem with Thanksgiving. There are a lot of problems this year. It used to be the Gunch tradition to have Thanksgiving at my house. This year we got a choice of having a picnic on the Murphy's oil spill where my house used to be or go somewheres else. It has to be somewhere with a lot of space. There are a lot of Gunches, and they ain't the minimalist type.

And then it turns out everybody got pressing plans on the actual day—what with in-laws and football games and suing insurance companies. We could just cancel it, but this is the wrong year for that. We better be grateful. We don't want to get on God's bad side again.

So we decide to get together three weeks early at my daughter Gumdrop's. She and her husband Slime and my grandbaby Lollipop and my mother-in-law Ms. Larda are staying in Folsom, in what used to be Slime's parents' vacation house.

Now we got the time and the place. The last problem is what we will eat.

Finally we decide to make it a potluck Thanksgiving. Then everybody can eat what they themselves bring; plus the turkey, which ain't a problem now that the men of the family have discovered it is manly to deep-fry that outside; and the dressing, which my mother-in-law Ms. Larda always makes.

Then the night before, Ms. Larda calls up. Her oyster stuffing is the best food God ever created but three people in a row called to tell her they can't eat it unless she takes out the breadcrumbs, and the onion, and the oysters. She says she can't cook under these new rules. I got to fix the stuffing.

So I got a choice between finding a all-night food store that has enough employees to actually be open all night, and then buying God-knows-what to suit everybody's taste, or making stuffing out of what I got, and let them take it or leave it.

I look in my fridge and I see, besides ice cubes, a

bottle of pina colada mix my gentleman friend Lust brought me back in August. (He was dropping hints about a lei, so I invited him over to watch Blue Hawaii.) In my cupboard I got a couple cans of crushed pineapple, Rice-A-Roni, and a bunch of little bags of cashews my friend Awlette gave me when I met her plane from Chicago.

I decide we are going to have Hawaiian pineapple stuffing with this turkey.

Well, the Gunch family arrives for Thanksgiving dinner looking at each other as lovingly as Al Copeland and Luann Hunter. While the men are in the back yard with the beer and turkey, I pour wine from a big box Lust brought for the ladies to sip. He even brought sparkling apple juice for Gumdrop and the kids.

So by the time they haul in the fried turkey, most of us are feeling pretty mellow. Which is a good thing, because we also got Gloriosa's tofu pie with whole wheat crust; Larva's bacon, ham, and sausage salad, and Gumdrop's big bowl of strained carrot and banana swirl topped with Froot Loops. Thank God we got plenty of beer and wine and apple juice to wash it down.

My Hawaiian stuffing turns out to be a hit. I had chopped up the cashews, mixed them with crushed pineapple and Rice-A-Roni, heated it up, and then poured the Pina Colada over it like a sauce. (Except for Gumdrop and the kids' portions, which I put pineapple juice on.) Everybody politely tastes all the other dishes, but they all (except Gumdrop) ask for seconds and thirds of the stuffing. Even Larva forgets it has carbs. I think the secret ingredient was the sauce, which I didn't realize had so much rum in it.

By the time dinner is over, we are all very cheerful. Some of us are so cheerful we spend the night on Gumdrop's living room floor, all together, just like we were for a couple months after Katrina. It brought back memories.

Maybe we got a new tradition here.

Fire in the Hole

This Christmas, I don't have to worry about what to buy for the person who has everything. Everybody I know got nothing.

My mother-in-law, Ms. Larda, says she could use a sack of grout and some roofing nails, and her sons, Leech and Lurch, who are working on her house that got flooded, want a lot of Blistex and some Therma-care back pain wraps.

Ms. Larda is going stir crazy in the wide-open spaces of the Northshore countryside, where she is staying with my daughter Gumdrop; but she can't come home until her house is fixed. It is a double, and Leech and Lurch live there too.

Anyway, the Gunches decided to exchange presents a little early, so I drove up there last week with all their packages gift-wrapped from Home Depot, including some Shake-a-Way urine-based raccoon repellant for Gumdrop, since she is a country girl now.

But for my grandbaby, Lollipop, I scored a Tickle Me Extreme Elmo, the little Sesame Street doll that giggles out loud. Gumdrop says this is the must-have gift for every two-year-old that got a TV.

It is almost dark when I pull up in the driveway that leads to their cabin in the woods, but I see Gumdrop's husband, Slime, and my brothers-in-law, Leech and Lurch, sitting in lawn chairs arranged in a circle next to the tool shed. They look like a prayer group, except they all got beers in their hands and shotguns across their laps. Whatever they are doing, I don't want to be no part of, so I just quietly walk across the yard toward the house.

Then I hear Leech ask if anybody wants another beer while he is up, and he sets down his shotgun and comes my way, so I ask him what is going on. He says they are guarding a skunk hole and they are going to shoot this skunk as soon as it shows its face.

Now, I don't know nothing about guns and less about skunks, but this don't seem too smart to me. Of course, none of them three are the sharpest tacks in the tire, if you get what I mean.

I decide to tell Gumdrop about it, but as soon as I open the door, her cat Rocky bolts outside. Now, Rocky is a indoor cat, because he don't got no claws.

But every now and then, he dashes for freedom. He also has long black fur, like a skunk.

I call "Rocky's out!" so them gun-happy skunk-hunters don't start blasting. Leech, who is a few steps behind me, says "There he is! There he is! There he is!" and rushes into the tool shed—which is strange, being as I have already scooped up Rocky.

A second later, Leech come tearing back out of there, bellowing "Skunnnk!"

This causes Lurch and Slime to jump up real quick, spilling their beers, and fire into the hole.

Maybe that's where the expression "fire in the hole" comes from.

I guess the shotgun pellets bounced back at them. Next thing I know, Lurch and Slime are jumping around clutching various parts of their legs. A skunk—I notice he does look like Rocky, a little—is streaking off toward the woods, and Leech is rolling around in the grass. I guess he got sprayed.

At least Leech isn't hurt, thank God, because the ambulance attendants won't let him anywhere near when they come to take Lurch and Slime away. One of them tells him to mix up hydrogen peroxide and baking soda and dishwashing soap and soak in it for about a year.

After they drive away, with Gumdrop following in her car, Ms. Larda mixes up a batch of what they said and brings it out in a bucket. Leech slinks into the tool shed to wash off and throws his clothes out the window. Afterwards, Ms. Larda goes out to smell him. She decides he ain't ready for the house yet, so she brings him a beanbag chair to sleep in. It is really Rocky's beanbag chair, but he will settle for the couch tonight.

Finally Gumdrop comes home with the other two, all patched up. They will be all right, but they been better. Slime goes right to bed and Lurch goes to the blow-up mattress in the spare room.

Gumdrop looks ready to cry. Some Christmas celebration: she just spent three hours in the emergency room and her uncle Leech is stinking up the tool shed. She could use a glass of wine, or three, but she can't have any because she is pregnant.

Pregnant or not, she needs some heavy-duty stuff. So I throw caution to the winds. I bring out the TMX Elmo for Lollipop. And he starts giggling, and Lollipop starts giggling along with him. Then I got to snicker, and Ms. Larda gets to cackling, and finally Gumdrop is laughing too. When Ms. Larda gets her breath back, she says that this skunk obviously has more brains than all three of them Elmer Fudd wannabes, because he expanded his hole up through the tool shed and was on his way out when Leech mistook him for Rocky. And then we guffaw for another ten minutes.

Then Ms. Larda remembers something. She goes outside and pokes Leech's clothes onto the end of a broomstick, and she marches over to the leaf pile down the hill, with Gumdrop and me and Lollipop and Elmo following behind, at a distance. She drops them in. Then she drops in a match.

We all stand upwind to watch the flames. It's kind of like a smaller and smellier version of them Christmas Eve fires they light on the bayou.

Elmo giggles, and that starts the rest of us off again. We stare at the fire and laugh until our sides hurt.

You don't have to have everything to have a merry Christmas.

GarGoyle's Delusions of Manliness

My mother-in-law, Ms. Larda, is back home in Chalmette.

Not a minute too soon. She says she can't never show her face in Folsom again.

She had been staying there on the Northshore with my daughter Gumdrop while her house was getting fixed after Katrina. Thank God it's ready.

What happened was, last Wednesday she got up at 5:30 A.M. in Folsom and went to make her coffee, like she does every morning, only this morning there ain't no coffee left in the canister. Nobody else in the house drinks coffee except Gumdrop, and she can't do that now that she is pregnant again.

Now, Gumdrop lives out in the country, five minutes by car from downtown Folsom, which has a traffic light, a feed 'n' seed store, and Gus's restaurant, open early for breakfast, no credit extended.

My son Gargoyle is on his Christmas vacation from LSU and since my apartment is small and he takes up a lot of space, he is vacationing on Gumdrop's couch. So Ms. Larda goes to the couch and inquires if she can borrow his car to go get some coffee. He don't say nothing, being as he won't be conscious for another five or six hours, so she takes that as a yes and picks up his keys off the end table and drives off.

While she is on her way, she notices that Gargoyle left a big old LSU 16-ounce insulated mug with a lid on it, right there in the cup holder. Sixteen ounces ought to be enough to hold her for awhile. She will just go to Gus's and get it filled and be back before Gumdrop's two-year-old, Lollipop, wakes up. Ms. Larda likes to get her up and settled in front of the TV with her bowl of Sugar Clumps so her mama can sleep late. This is the least she can do for having a place to live ever since she got too fat for the FEMA trailer.

But there is something she don't know about that insulated mug. Evidently there was some kind of safe sex week up at LSU and they had a bowl of what I will call "safe sex items" in little foil packets setting out on a table, free. My son must have happened to walk past there when he had his empty mug in his hand and dumped most of the bowl into his mug. He must have had a time squishing them all down, but he did, and then he screwed this lid on. And he threw the mug in his car. What kind of plans he had God only knows, and God probably don't want to think about it.

Flash forward to Ms. Larda. She scurries into Gus's, and she sees a couple of people she met at St. John, the Catholic church there, who are already polishing off their eggs and grits. She smiles and wishes them a good morning, hard as it is to be nice to anybody before her coffee. Ms. Larda has the feeling that they think anybody from New Orleans is a little weird, so she is glad she at least put on some lipstick and brushed her hair before she left the house, so she looks halfway decent.

She pays the waitress for 16 ounces of coffee, and goes to take the lid off the mug, but it is stuck. After she struggles with it a while, the waitress tries to help, but she can't pry it off either.

Finally the gentleman from the church gets up, and says, "May I?" and he wrenches it. Pop! Off it comes. And all these safe sex items that have been compressed in that mug ever since Safe Sex Week spring out every which way.

Ms. Larda lets out a shriek, naturally, because she is startled, and then she sees what has landed all over the floor, and she knows that if these country folks thought she was weird, now they got proof.

But I got to say, she has fast reactions for a old lady with no coffee in her. She don't look at the waitress or the church people or anybody else. She sets the LSU mug down on the counter and says, "I think I'll use a Styrofoam cup." And she pours her coffee and steps over the safe sex items like they was roaches and walks out with her head held high.

Back at Gumdrop's, she stomps over to the couch and kicks it a bunch of times. Nothing on the couch moves, so she goes ahead and gets Lollipop up. Then she starts packing for home.

I never would have known about all this if Gargoyle hadn't called the next day asking if I had seen his LSU mug. Ms. Larda and I happen to be having coffee ourselves at the time, and I say to her that he sure seemed upset about a $5 mug. She says to tell him if he wants that cup so bad, he can go out back and dig in Gumdrop's compost heap. I say, "Is that where it is?" and she says, "No, but since he wants to make his grandmother look like a dirty old woman, he can wallow around in some dirt himself."

Then she tells me about them people in Folsom thinking she is a sex fiend. She can hear it now— "carrying God knows how many safe sex items in her coffee cup, at her age. Never too late, in New Orleans . . ." and they'll just laugh, real nasty.

She gets up and pours us both another cup of coffee, but this time she adds a splash of Kahlua.

"It's good to be home, Modine," she says.

Here's to that.

When All Else Fails—
Alleluia!

Most people in New Orleans have a tradition for Carnival Day—circling their ladders on St. Charles Avenue, or riding a truck behind the Rex parade, or walking from the French Quarter to wherever the parade is.

My daughter Gumdrop has a new Carnival tradition. She has babies.

She done it twice now. Last time, back in 2005, she was dressed like a apple on a stick and she had to get down off a truck float on Napoleon Avenue and waddle over to Baptist Memorial to have my grandbaby Lollipop.

This time she didn't even make it to the parade. She and her husband Slime are living up north of the lake and they were coming across the Causeway to meet up with the rest of the Gunches on St. Charles when she started with her pains. So they headed for the closest hospital, East Jefferson in Metairie. And before I could get there through the parade traffic, I had a grandson.

And Gumdrop lost her bet.

The baby was supposed to be named Bernard, after the Parish. But my son Gargoyle bet her that this baby would be born on Mardi Gras. If he lost, he would personally provide 12 Saturday nights of free babysitting.

But if he won, he would get to name the baby.

Gumdrop figured the odds were astronomical against her having two babies on Carnival Day. So she took the bet.

Which is why my grandson is named Go-Cup.

Gargoyle said if Gumdrop wanted, she could call him Geaux-Cup, but she said that is too Uptown for her taste.

And since we are Catholics, the next thing we got to do is get him baptized. My mother-in-law, Ms. Larda, is worried because Go-Cup ain't the name of any saint she knows of, and sometimes priests are picky about naming babies after saints. Also, she got it in her head that he should be baptized in St. Louis Cathedral in the French Quarter, since I am temporarily living there now, in a apartment behind my gentleman friend Lust's bar, the Sloth Lounge.

This is our chance for the Gunch family to show

some class, she says to me. So she has been making me go pick her up and bring her to Mass at the cathedral every Sunday, so they will get to know us there.

Well, they know us all right.

Last Saturday, we two spent the evening sorting throws for Annual Sloth St. Patrick's Parade. My gentleman friend Lust owns the Sloth and he said he would treat us to red beans and rice. Now, when Ms. Larda cooks red beans, she is very careful to prick every single bean with a pin beforehand, so nobody gets no problems. But Lust ordered these beans from Popeyes' and they are what you call potent.

And because of St. Patrick's Day, we had cabbage on the side.

Next day, we still have problems.

"Just call me Katrina, Modine, I got enough wind," she says to me on our way to Mass the next morning. "Not to be undelicate." I tell her I feel like Rita, myself.

We walk into the cathedral, and she says, "They been burning incense, thanks be to God. We will just sit in the back and hope we don't disturb nobody."

God got other plans. This usher rushes up and whispers that one of the ladies who was supposed to do the reading from scripture didn't show up. He looks at Ms. Larda and says he has seen her there at lot, and he knows she will be happy to do the readings for the day. This means she is supposed to stand up there in the pulpit in front of the entire congregation and read some scripture passages out loud.

Now, Ms. Larda ain't in no condition to be any-where near a microphone, and while she is thinking of a mannerly way to explain that, he says, "Thanks and God bless" and scampers away.

So she digs out a roll of Tums and pops one in her mouth. "Say a quick prayer to Our Lady of Prompt Succor," she says. "Sometimes she works faster than Tums."

But neither of them comes through in time. So she walks up to the front and stands a little way back from the microphone. She clears her throat, real soft, but the "ahem" bounces around the walls like thunder.

And then she starts reading from Jeremiah: "In the year King Uzziah died, I saw the Lord seated on a high and lofty throne . . ."

I got to say she looks real dignified, and she got a powerful voice.

". . . with the trains of his garment filling the temple . . ."

She is reading faster and faster. That ain't a good sign.

"Seraphim were stationed above . . . ALLELU-LIAALLELUIA!"

I jump and I notice other people looking startled. "Alleluia" ain't in the script. But everybody automatically sings "Alleluia" back at her. She reads another couple of lines and then she roars out "Alleluia" again, and everybody alleluias back. By the end she has worked four more alleluias into the one reading;

the people in the pews are wide awake and Ms. Larda looks like she feels much better.

Afterward, we are slinking out the cathedral and into Jackson Square. And Ms. Larda is furiously whispering that this is Lent, and you are never supposed to say "alleluia" in church because alleluia is joyful and Lent is sad, but she was desperate . . . Then I see the usher running up behind us. He says Father wants us to know what a lively service that was, and he certainly wants Ms. Larda back for the Easter services when her expressions of joy will be an appropriate inspiration for the congregation.

Ms. Larda thanks him, and we hurry away.

"Our Lady of Prompt Succor came through," she says to me. "You never know how your prayers will be answered."

Amen, and pass the Beano.

Solution to Shrinkage

This is a story about king cake shrinkage.

Now, a king cake is the easiest cake in the world to sneak a slice of without nobody knowing.

If you cut a wedge out of a regular cake without asking, you are in trouble—especially if it was for birthday party purposes or something like that.

But a king cake is a big rambling oval, only one skinny layer high. All you got to do is cut yourself a sliver, pull it out, and then force the edges back together and smear the icing to cover up the cut.

Not that you personally would ever do it.

And if that don't work—if maybe you cut your slice too big and you can't force the edges to come together—you got to fall back on your high school geometry. You calculate the exact opposite place on the other side of the oval, and take out the same size slice on that side. Then you can push that cake back together, and nobody will know.

But you got to eat the slices you stole immediately, before you put the cake back together, so in case you got the slice the plastic baby is in—which you probably will because God is watching and he won't approve— you can slip that back before you fix the cake.

And you can't do it more than once on the same cake. Two slices maximum. Otherwise, somebody is going to notice the shrinkage.

Now you would think my brothers-in-law Lurch and Leech would understand that, as many cakes as they have personally shrunk. But even experienced experts can get distracted by lady mud wrestlers with large bosoms.

And that's what happened to them.

Now that they have moved back into their double house in Chalmette, my mother-in-law Ms. Larda and whatever old friends—mostly widow ladies, like her— have washed up nearby, have started holding king cake parties at each other's houses or trailers every week; dancing to old Vince Vance albums and talking about what's gone (everything) and what's not (Metairie). Ms. Larda got the baby in the cake last week, so it is her turn. She went all the way out to Randazzo's in Metairie for one of their super-sized king cakes.

She brings it home, and then she thinks of the million and one other things she needs before the ladies come, and she is just getting ready to tear out of the house when Leech shows up at the door and says he and Lurch need to watch a important wrestling match on her TV because theirs isn't working, so she says fine. But knowing them, she runs back in the laundry room behind the kitchen and leaves the king cake on the ironing board. Them boys have never looked at a ironing board in their lives, so she figures this is safe.

Wrong, of course. Them two have a sense of smell like basset hounds, and she ain't a block away before they have sniffed it out.

Anyway, they set it on the coffee table, and they start watching the show, and they cut a little slice here, and a matching slice there, and another slice here . . .

Thank God I show up early, because when I walk in and ask what they think they are doing, they got it down to the size of a glazed doughnut.

There's no time to get to Randazzo's. Or anywhere else.

Like they say, desperation is the mother of all inventions. They got 20 minutes until party time.

They run back to their side of the house and come back with three boxes of Hostess Twinkies, which they always keep a stash of in case of a food emergency. Leech asks me to find a knife; and then he asks for the sugar. And then he wants to know if Ms. Larda got any food coloring, which she does, and then he roots through the refrigerator and grabs a squeeze bottle of grape jelly.

Then Lurch, precise as a surgeon, slices a Twinkie lengthwise, halfway up, and forms it into a Y, and shoves another Twinkie into the arms of the Y, and then cuts the bottom half of that into a Y, and so on, until he got a chain of Twinkies looking like braided dough, sort of. Meanwhile, Lurch mixes yellow food coloring with sugar in one coffee cup, and green food coloring with sugar in another cup. They arrange the braided-looking Twinkies into a big oval in the Randazzo's box, fill in the gaps between Twinkies with grape jelly, and then dump the colored sugar all over it—at the last minute they remember to stick the baby in—and voila!—it does look like a purple, green, and gold king cake.

"Presentation is everything," Lurch says to me with a straight face.

Excuuuuuse me.

Now the most I have ever seen either Leech or Lurch do in regards to food preparation is to remove the peel off a banana before they eat it.

But they must have fell asleep with the Food Channel on for a few nights.

Ms. Larda rushes in and starts laying out little triangle sandwiches and healthful vegetables with unhealthful dip; and then the ladies arrive, and there is a lot of talking and chomping. Lurch and Leech beat it out the back door.

Then Ms. Larda opens the Randazzo's box and

frowns. "I asked for their traditional cake," she says. But she shrugs and starts slicing.

It is delicious, because in addition to the maybe 5,000 calories worth of filling in the middle of every Twinkie, it also got colored sugar and grape jelly.

Maybe them boys got a undiscovered talent. You got to wonder what they could do with Moon Pies.

Gorgeous But Trashy

My mother-in-law, Ms. Larda, is usually so busy minding other people's business she don't think about herself. But now she got a problem. She decides to ask for advice from her daughter Gloriosa, because this problem involves money, and Gloriosa is the only one in the family who never hits her up for any, being as she married rich.

So Ms. Larda bakes a batch of carrot muffins—Gloriosa's children ain't allowed to have real junk food—and goes Uptown to see her. She gives a muffin to each of the kids, who ain't too grateful, being as they always hope for doughnuts, and shoos them out of the kitchen, and sits down to have a mother-daughter chat.

She is just dunking her first muffin—which she wishes was a doughnut—and deciding how to start this conversation, when Gloriosa starts unloading her own problem. The thing is, Gloriosa really got no problems. She come through Katrina with a house and a high income and everybody alive. But no, that ain't enough. Her life is miserable, she says, because of the garbage police who have taken over Keeping Our City Tidy. Every household in New Orleans has been issued a garbage bin and the occupants are required to use it. By law.

Ms. Larda, being as she lives in St. Bernard, just outside New Orleans, says she don't see no problem with a free garbage bin, and to tell you the truth, New Orleans has needed tidying up for a long time.

Gloriosa says this garbage bin is not only ugly, it is so big it comes up to her boobs and so heavy she can't pull it around front once she puts the garbage in it. So she got to make one trip all the way from the back yard and down the driveway dragging the empty garbage bin, and then two or three more trips with the actual garbage to put in it, and it is just tooo much.

So keep this bin on the front lawn, says Ms. Larda. Put it off to one side a little. Well, she should have known better than to suggest THAT.

Gloriosa is a lawn Nazi. She has grass you can comb; she has hedges clipped so perfect they would make a French poodle jealous; she has matching azalea bushes on each side of her steps that bloom twice a year in perfect unison and know better than to drop their dead flowers on her front walk; and along the side of the yard, she has a straight row of very well-behaved elephant ear plants. They don't droop and they don't spread and when Gloriosa comes along, they stand at attention.

And now this blot on her perfect landscape.

Now, Ms. Larda has a real problem. She retired from her last job in the foundations department at Krauss years ago, and up until Katrina she got along fine on her savings and social security and what she inherited from Mr. Gunch. But rebuilding the house used all that up; the insurance company she been paying all these years is hemming and hawing about paying her back, and she ain't holding her breath waiting for Road Home payments. She got what Gloriosa—if she shut up long enough to listen—would call a cash flow problem. Ms. Larda literally don't have a pot to (ahem!) in. She bought one of them new ecologically correct low-flow toilets, and it has turned out to be no-flow. But she can't afford a plumber.

She knows she has to calm Gloriosa down before she can talk about this. The two of them go outside and stand in front of the garbage bin. "What you need is a way to disguise this bin; make it less obvious so you can keep it on the front lawn," Ms. Larda says.

It so happens that she has been driving around

with a bag of old clothes in her trunk, hoping to pass by a Salvation Army store or somewhere that is accepting donations. So she roots through the bag, and she pulls out one of the muumuus she wore while we was evacuated at Orange Beach.

Ms. Larda is the hefty type, and she says there ain't a bathing suit ever been designed that will flatter her figure, so this is what she wore instead. It comes up to just below her armpits and is gathered there with elastic, and the print looks sort of like elephant ears. She takes it and wrestles it over the garbage bin. It is a perfect fit. Gloriosa runs to her back shed and comes out with a enormous straw hat and they plunk it on top the lid, and voila, a eyesore turns into a thing of—maybe not beauty, but not too bad. It blends in, especially when Gloriosa drags it into the line of elephant ears along the side fence.

They are standing there feeling proud of themselves, when Gloriosa's neighbor Bitsy Boswell strolls over and says she would give $50 if she had one like that for her garbage bin. "Sold!" says Ms. Larda. And she roots out one with a azalea print and they put that one on Bitsy's bin.

And just like that, Larda Gunch's Garbage Gowns Ltd is born. And not only do people want gowns to match their gardens, but them people who love to put up wreaths and flags for every holiday see a whole new way to one-up the neighbors. So she starts a new line for different holidays—her Halloween designs are coming out soon. Lucky she is talented with sewing.

So now she got enough cash flow to take care of the no-flow. And if that's the only flow problem she has to worry about this hurricane season, she'll be happy. Won't we all.

Private Collection

I am trapped in my mother-in-law's garage.

It could happen to anybody. I knock at Ms. Larda's front door and nobody answers. I see her garage door standing wide open, so I go in that way, thinking maybe she is in her kitchen, which is in the back, and can't hear me. The door between the garage and kitchen is locked, but there is a little doorbell right there, so I press it.

Come to find out, this ain't no doorbell; it is the automatic garage door closer. But I don't know that at the time.

When I hear the garage door lurch downward, I shriek and try to run out. I am too late. So I run back to the kitchen door and pound on it. Chopsley, her Chihuahua, has a hissy fit inside, but nobody else comes.

I try to push up the garage door with my hands,

but it won't budge. I flick the switch next to it to make it automatically go back up again. This turns the back yard light on and off, but I don't know that, neither. I think the door is broken.

I got to explain. Ms. Larda just got her house rebuilt, with a garage next to her kitchen. And, of course, she got a automatic garage door opener.

My opinion is, nobody needs a automatic garage door opener, because nobody needs to open their garage door, unless they keep their car in there, which they don't, because it won't fit along with the junk they also got in there—unless they are maybe Donald Trump, who can probably afford a separate storage unit.

But Ms. Larda ain't Donald Trump, and even though Katrina cleaned out all her old junk, in two years she has accumulated plenty more.

Besides which, she is in business creating decorative garbage bin muumuus for people in New Orleans who don't like the looks of the new garbage bins that the city strictly requires all residents to use. (I think they should strictly require all residents to stop shooting each other, but don't get me started on THAT.)

Anyway, she also uses the garage to store her fabric and artificial flowers and like that.

And last week she asks would I pick up some feathery masks at a costume shop near my apartment. She needs them for a special Mardi Gras muumuu for some Carnival bigwig's garbage bin.

I got plenty enough to do, but you don't tell Ms. Larda no, so I find time to get the masks and run them over to her house.

And here I am.

I pound on the kitchen door some more, and that sets Chopsley off again, but still nobody comes.

I am going to be here a while. I rummage around and find a lawn chair and make myself comfortable. There ain't no windows in Ms. Larda's garage, but there is a light on. And Ms. Larda installed a little room air conditioner for Chopsley, so she can lock him out there when she has a repairman or somebody in the house that he don't approve of. So I turn that on.

I got plenty of time to think. My first thought is that the automatic garage door opener must have been invented by a man.

And this man, whoever he was, probably also had the brilliant idea to install washers and dryers in garages. So some self-respecting lady like myself would be doing laundry in my own garage, and would decide to take off what I was wearing and wash that too— just to get everything done—and would be standing there stark naked, measuring out the detergent, when somebody—I never found out who—would press the door-open button and I would have to streak out clutching the Tide box to cover my personal parts.

And I can only thank God that happened before YouTube was invented.

Why didn't this genius invent something that

would do good in the world, like house keys that come when you call them, or a car that finds its own parking space? I ask you that.

I pound on the door some more, and Chopsley gets all worked up again, but still nobody comes.

I am facing a refrigerator with "FEMA THIS!" spray-painted on the front. My brothers-in-law Lurch and Leech rescued it when somebody left it on the curb after the storm. They cleaned it with bleach, and now it keeps their emergency beer stash. I take a bottle of Abita Amber and sit back down.

Then I see a cardboard box labeled "trashy books." It is full of—well, well, well—romance novels. So Ms. Larda has a secret vice. I sit back and I sip this beer and start reading about bosoms that heave and members that throb.

A couple hours later, I been through three beers and a whole lot of heaving and throbbing. Meanwhile Ms. Larda, who, it turns out, was asleep on the couch without her hearing aids in, wakes up and shuffles into the kitchen, where Chopsley is growling at the door. She opens it, sees a human being, and lets loose a screech. I fling up my book and screech back. We stare at each other. Then I rush past her to the bathroom.

Afterwards, I explain, in kind of a snippy way, that I been trapped there because her automatic garage door opener don't work. She pushes the little door-bell by the kitchen door, and the garage door lurches right up.

Oh.

I got to say something to save face. So I say, "You got a nice library out there, Ms. Larda." And I smirk. But she just rolls her eyes.

"I'm going to add to it," she says. "Garage Door Openers for Dummies."

I guess I could write it.

Nervous Christmas Sock

It is dark. I have grease on my new red velvet slacks from crawling around looking under trucks for a Chihuahua in a monkey suit. I ain't in the Christmas spirit.

But I got a Christmas story to tell.

It all started because, like everybody knows, Christmas has got all out of hand. I blame that on people who do their shopping early. They rush out and buy something for everybody in creation, right down to their gas meter reader. But when they are finished, they can't stop. It's like painting one wall of a room—you got to keep on painting. So they do more Christmas stuff. This is why we see nine-foot Santa Clauses constructed entirely out of colored toothpicks on lawns in Metairie.

Well, my mother-in-law Ms. Larda is one of them.

This year, she even made sock monkeys with her own hands for all the little kids in the family, so she don't have to worry about giving them some toy that their parents will take away immediately because it might be made from toxins in China. And she still finishes three weeks before Halloween.

I thought she would have plenty to keep her busy with her garbage bin decorating business, but no. She put the finishing touches on her last Mr. Bingle garbage bin muumuu in the first week of November. Then she decorates every square inch of her house with toy soldiers and Santa Clauses and fat little angels. Then she sets up a inflatable nativity scene on the front lawn.

She looks around for what to do next. And she sees Chopsley, her little Chihuahua. She gets a brilliant idea. She makes him a sock monkey costume. When she tries it on him, he looks just like a sock monkey, except he bites.

I got to explain about Chopsley. His main activity is sitting and shaking, unless somebody walks into the room, when his main activity is not getting stepped on. If he was a cat, he would act real cool about it—just lounge in everybody's way and give them a cold stare. But Chihuahuas are a lot more nervous. Chopsley's method of not getting stepped on is to yap constantly so you know he's there.

She dresses him in this monkey suit for her Christmas in Chalmette party, which is the next thing she decides to do. I come with my gentleman friend Lust, and all the Gunches come with their kids, and all her old friends who are still around, and all three of the neighbors who have moved back on her block come too.

That's a lot of feet for Chopsley to worry about. Lust's are the worst because they are big, plus Lust is a little deaf and can't hear high-pitched sounds, like the ones Chopsley makes all the time. He is Chopsley's worst nightmare.

I am helping Ms. Larda set out the eats, and Lust is jabbering with somebody about the Saints, and this conversation involves some foot stomping. This pushes Chopsley over the edge. I glance over and see him chomp on Lust's pants leg. Lust don't even notice. He just swings his leg like an elephant would if a fly tickled him, and poor Chopsley sails across the kitchen. My brother-in-law Leech, walking in with a red velvet cake, almost trips over him. We all rush to catch the cake and forget about Chopsley.

Later, Ms. Larda notices his yapping has stopped, but she assumes I have shut him in her bedroom, which is what I usually do when Lust is around.

Finally, after all the people with kids have gone home, and the rest of us are squeezing out what's left in the wine box, Ms. Larda realizes her bedroom door is open. Chopsley ain't there.

She has a awful thought. What if Chopsley was knocked out, and got sent home with one of the kids instead of their sock monkey? A sock monkey that wakes up and bites would be even worse than a toy from China that shouldn't be ingested.

So we start making phone calls, and we get a lot of hysteria from parents (parents are more nervous than Chihuahuas these days) but come to find out, all the sock monkeys that went home really are sock monkeys.

Chopsley is lost.

He ain't in the house, so he must be outside. Now, in his whole life, Chopsley has only gone outside when he has to do his business in the back yard, and even then, Ms. Larda keeps an eye on him because if the grass is too high he gets lost in it. So he ain't what you call street smart. And now he is wandering around them abandoned houses, facing rats and snakes and mold spores bigger than him.

Ms. Larda is so upset, we all get upset too, even though this has been the most peaceful party we have had at her house in years.

I call nine-one-one. The operator says, "A Chihuahua in a monkey suit? Uhhh-HUH!" She ain't going to be no help.

So we swarm outside to search with flashlights.

No luck. Lust blames himself, and even though he don't got no love lost for Chopsley, he feels bad.

Finally everybody has left but me, looking under parked trucks, and Lust, checking out the nativity scene.

Then I hear a yell, and it ain't "Merry Christmas!"

A sock monkey is clamped on Lust's ankle. He found Chopsley.

We must have passed that manger 10 or 12 times before Lust noticed it was shaking.

Chopsley did leave a souvenir there. There was probably a few of them in the original manger too, being as it was occupied by animals and a baby, Lust says. Ms. Larda cleans it up, after she clutches Chopsley to her bosom and promises never to make him wear a monkey suit again.

So it turned out to be a merry Christmas story after all.

Little Booger

When I was little, I thought somebody three feet high and disguised in a bedsheet was extremely scary. So that is what I wore on Halloween, and I always collected enough candy to make myself sick.

My own kids wanted something fancier, so I cut black plastic garbage bags into bat wings and taped them on with duct tape. They flapped around the neighborhood until their wings fell off. Then it was time to go home and eat the haul.

Now parents pay good money over the Internet for designer costumes that look adorable for at least 15 minutes, until they are smeared with Tootsie Roll slobber.

I notice the little boys usually wear something scary, the grosser the better. But the girls—with NO exceptions whatsoever—dress like princesses, and it don't matter if their grandmother explains until she is blue in the face that on Halloween you are supposed to dress scary and princesses ain't scary. Not on purpose, anyway.

They wear tiaras and sparkly dresses that are pink or lavender. Those are the only colors princesses are allowed to wear. I know that from my granddaughter Lollipop. She is going on three, so she is a expert.

I told my daughter Gumdrop it is more creative to whip up your costume on the spot with whatever is lying around. But she says things have changed, and going on the Internet is creative enough for her.

A lot has changed, all right. Halloween ain't just one night any more. People are running around dressed weird for the entire month—except where I live, in the French Quarter. There they dress weird for the entire year.

Anyway, last week there is this big pre-Halloween family festival out in the country near Gumdrop's house. There is going to be a costume contest and she entered my two grandbabies. Now this costume contest is completely different than the costume contests in the Quarter, which have all them transformers prancing around in their high heels. This is a wholesome family-oriented costume contest, and Gumdrop thinks it is a chance to make a good impression on her new neighbors.

Lollipop is going to be a princess, of course. Her

little brother Go-Cup is only eight months old and way too cute to be anything scary. So Gumdrop decides to dress him as Winnie-the-Pooh. Well, that is tempting fate.

So she orders outfits for both kids, with a sparkly dress and tiara for Lollipop and a furry suit with ears for Go-Cup.

Grown-ups get in free if they are in costume too, so she orders herself a tail and some pointy ears, so she can say she is a kitty cat. Her husband Slime decides to go with a Shrek mask and green skin. In case you don't know, Shrek is that movie cartoon ogre that little boys love because he passes gas and picks his feet and his nose and does other disgusting things. Gumdrop tells him he can dress like Shrek, but if he acts like Shrek at the festival, she will NOT be amused.

She asks would I come take pictures, so I throw on my witch costume, and count on the fact that I just got a real bad haircut to complete my look.

The contestants are divided into age groups, and each child is supposed to walk across the stage while the announcer says, "And what is this little goblin?" And the child is supposed to say "Dragon," or "Princess," or "Elmo," or "Princess," or "Pirate," or "Princess," or whatever they are. But mostly they burst into tears, so after a while, the mamas start walking up with them. After that, they are supposed to stay on the stage, form a line, and wait for judging. Well. I am glad I'm not a judge. Those costumes are something else, and obviously none of them were made by loving hands at home.

Lollipop is in the toddler category and Go-Cup is in the infant class, immediately following. When Lollipop is called, Gumdrop hands the baby to Slime and walks Lollipop up on the stage, while I scurry to the front with the camera.

Slime tells me later what happened: just as he is realizing Gumdrop still has the diaper bag on her arm, disaster strikes. To put it delicately, Winnie-the-Pooh lives up to his name, and his diaper and his costume ain't no match for what he lets loose. Slime holds him out at arm's length and rushes to the restroom, peels off his entire outfit and washes him clean. Clean, but naked.

There is a crumpled-up brown paper grocery bag lying on the counter, that somebody must have used to bring their costume in.

I am still at the foot of the stage with my camera, bumping elbows with competing grandmothers, when I hear them call Go-Cup's name. Nothing happens. From the stage, Gumdrop evidently sees Slime's Shrek mask in the crowd, because she motions for him to get himself up there. And Slime does, clutching Go-Cup, with his fuzzy head and his fat little arms sticking out of a crumpled brown bag. The announcer says, "And what is THIS little goblin?" Slime looks blank, and then he says, "A booger?"

Gumdrop is ready to die. She breaks out of line

and snatches her baby-in-a-bag. Then the announcer says, "Oho! A family theme!" Well, these people are very, very big on family togetherness, and they assume this family coordinated their costumes on purpose: turns out a cat and a princess are both characters in the Shrek movie, and Go-Cup is dressed as the appropriate Shrek accessory.

So they win a whole basket of stuff donated by local merchants. The other parents ain't too happy that their expensive costumes were beat by a paper bag, but I think there's a lesson in that.

Things haven't changed so much after all.

What's That Joke About Parsley?

It's a good thing God put Thanksgiving at the end of the hurricane season. Then we know for sure whether we got reason to be thankful or not.

The Gunch family is taking a chance and celebrating it a couple weeks early this year, because my brothers-in-law Leech and Lurch got jobs at the Fairgrounds, so they have to work on the actual Thanksgiving Day.

For our Thanksgiving dinner, usually the men deep-fry the turkey in the yard, with a TV out there so they can watch football, and we each bring our own specialty to make up the rest of the meal. Last year we did it at my daughter Gumdrop's.

But this year my sister-in-law Gloriosa invited her husband Proteus's parents, old Mr. Proteus and Ms.

Sarcophaga, to join us. They are high-society types, and I guess she don't want them to enter any of the hovels the rest of us call homes, so she is insisting we have dinner at her gorgeous big house Uptown.

Except for the fried turkey, she is cooking the whole meal herself. This is because Ms. Sarcophaga got indigestive problems. She is allergic to shellfish, nuts, and berries; caffeine and alcohol gives her the hot flashes; cheese gives her gas; grapefruit don't mix with her medication; and sugar is too fattening. But Gloriosa is determined to cook a dinner she can eat. She says it is going to be delicious. I got my doubts. Ms. Sarcophaga looks like she lives on artificially sweetened Styrofoam pellets.

Anyway, Gloriosa tells us not to bring any food to this dinner.

Well, we can't just show up with nothing. My mother-in-law, Ms. Larda, says she is going to bring a Autumn Harvest potpourri which comes in a little decorator bowl, and my daughter Gumdrop is bringing a arrangement of chrysanthemums and turkey feathers. My gentleman friend Lust and myself are bringing some of his best bourbon, from behind his bar in the Sloth Lounge.

My brothers-in-law Leech and Lurch show up early with nothing to donate, so Gloriosa gets them right to work chopping the ingredients for the mock oyster stuffing. She has this new granite island in the middle of the kitchen, and she set out bowls of all kinds of things Ms. Sarcophaga ain't allergic to. She tells them to chop everything. Then she goes out to her patio to oversee Proteus and the turkey.

Ms. Larda comes in, plunks her potpourri down in the kitchen and goes out on the patio to find somebody's business to stick her nose into. When Leech and Lurch finish chopping, they go out there too, because Lust is pouring all the men a few fingers of bourbon. And Proteus brought some oysters he don't want his mother to see (she gets sick if she as much as sees a oyster) and he drops them into the deep fryer with the turkey, and pretty soon they got fried oyster appetizers.

Then Gloriosa sautes everything the boys chopped with Progresso bread crumbs and butter to make stuffing, and puts it in a big pan in the oven. Gumdrop arranges her flowers and feathers on the table and tells the kids not to eat them. Proteus's parents show up with white wine. Old Mr. Proteus toddles outside with the men and the bourbon but Ms. Sarcophaga, who looks like she just got her face tightened, manages a smile and says that the aroma from the kitchen is wonderful.

And it is. Ms. Larda says the smell is good enough to bring back the dead with an appetite. Gloriosa says it must be the stuffing. She put fresh parsley in it. That don't go over big with Ms. Larda—she has always been the champion stuffing maker in the family—but she says she'll start adding fresh parsley too, if it makes that much difference. Old Mr. Proteus starts to babble some joke about parsley, but Ms. Sarcophaga shoots him a look and he snaps his mouth shut.

Now, the rest of us have already sneaked out to the patio and had a few fried oysters to cut our appetite, but Ms. Sarcophaga has not. By the time we sit down, she must be starving, because she digs in the second we finish grace. Then Gloriosa taps her glass and says she has a few people to thank, so we all put down our forks and look embarrassed. She thanks her mother- and father-in-law for the wine, and Lust for the bourbon, and Gumdrop for the arrangement. She starts to sit down and Ms. Larda says, "And my potpourri?"

Gloriosa says, "Potpourri?"

Ms. Larda says, "In the kitchen. On the island."

Leech says, "That was potpourri?"

Ms. Sarcophaga starts to gag.

Then a lot happens at once. Ms. Sarcophaga tears off to the bathroom. Leech says, "That wasn't the seasoning?" Ms. Larda grabs the potpourri bowl, which is now empty, and reads the label underneath: "Do not ingest." We all snatch the plates away from the kids and ask if they ate any. Come to find out, poor Sarcophaga was the only one who did, but she ate A LOT, judging by what we hear from the bathroom. Somebody calls 911.

I realize that, thanks to the bourbon, old Mr. Proteus ain't in no condition to fill out the 72 forms that are going to be required in the emergency room. Gloriosa and young Proteus are hysterically looking down their children's throats for signs of potpourri, so they ain't going to be no help. I climb in the ambulance and hold Ms. Sarcophaga's hand all the way over to the Touro Hospital emergency room.

While she is getting her stomach pumped, I get a Snickers out the snack machine. That's my Thanksgiving dinner.

And you know what? I am thankful anyway.

Come on Down!

It used to be, when people would call and tell me they was coming to New Orleans for their summer vacation, I would tell them that if they wanted steam and heat, they could stand in their shower. That would smell better.

Now I tell them to come on down.

This is not because the climate has changed since Katrina. It is because now I don't have to let them stay at my house, since I don't got a house no more.

My gentleman friend Lust owns the Sloth Lounge in the French Quarter, and me and my daughter Gladiola are in an apartment in the back, which got no room for visitors unless they want to sleep under the kitchen table with the dog.

When Aunt Chlorine called, I said she was welcome to stay in a hotel. And then I said maybe she could get the bellman to refer me some customers, being as I am in a new profession.

From her reaction, I guess I should have phrased that different.

Let me back up some. I had been working in nail design at my friend Awlette's Topsy Toesies beauty salon. But it turns out I am no Michelangelo when it comes to painting other people's toes. With all due respect, I bet the Sistine Chapel ceiling didn't squeal and jump and say it was ticklish. And it sure didn't have foot odor.

Anyway, a couple of my customers wound up with Shimmery Tangerine to the first knuckle. So Awlette decided that since my best talent is talking, I should just answer the phones. And for a while everything was fine and good.

Then I start getting calls from some guy with a foot fetish. I would answer, "Topsy Toesies, how can I help you?" and this man's voice would say, "Ooooh, baby, tell me you are wearing thong sandals," or some such. I couldn't tell him off because customers could hear, so I just hung up. Pretty soon I was so nervous I would hang up whenever anybody with a deep voice called. Unfortunately, a couple of our lady customers had deep cigarette voices and I hung up on them too. That ain't good for business, so I decided to find a different job.

Which means I got to look halfway decent. But I got another problem. All my pants are too tight. Now, I been a skinny Minnie my whole life, so this comes as a shock.

I talk about it to my sister-in-law Gloriosa, who is the Gunch family health expert being as she used to work in a doctor's office. She says I got the mid-life weight gain that comes right along with the hot flashes, which I also got. She says I got to tighten up my abs, which is what they call stomachs now, and turn them into a six-pack. I say I don't want no six-pack, or even a keg. I want this stomach to disappear entirely before I have to join the Sisterhood of the Elastic Pants. She rolls her eyes and says I probably need to lay off the Irish coffee at the Sloth Lounge and switch to diet green tea. And maybe I should take a nice long walk every day.

Well, one advantage to being unemployed is you got time to do what is good for you. The disadvantage is you got no money to do it with. But walking is free. So I walk.

One day, this woman in a floppy hat flounces past me, blathering away, and there are maybe 20 people following her, hanging on every word. She is a tour guide. She gets paid to walk and talk.

I can walk and talk. And my next hot flash is a light bulb going on over my head.

Well, it turns out you got to pass a history test and get a license from the New Orleans Taxicab Bureau—

for true—to walk people around on their own feet and point out the sights. But all that history I was forced to learn back at Celibacy Academy is finally coming in handy, because I actually know enough to pass this test.

And because of the green tea, I also know the location of every toilet in the French Quarter.

I get a tour agency to hire me on trial, and for my first tour, I am supposed to meet a bankers' convention group at Jackson Square.

But what I don't realize is that tourists don't know nothing about New Orleans, except that it is connected with boobs and beads. I go to Jackson Square. They go to Jax Brewery, which they think is Jackson Square.

So I stand in front the Andrew Jackson statue, and I wait. Then my cell phone rings.

I say, "Hello?" and I hear a lot of static and then "What are you wearing?" The foot fetish guy. Well. I forget I am a lady, and I screech and I insult his private parts, and I slam the phone back into my purse, feeling a lot better.

Then I wonder how he got my cell phone number.

You see where this is going. It was not the foot fetish guy. I have insulted the private parts of some bank president from Omaha standing in Jax Brewery trying to pick me out of the crowd. The tour agency had given him my cell phone number in case he had trouble locating me.

So much for that job.

But when I am crying in my green tea about it to Lust, he comes up with a brilliant idea.

Now I lead Sloth tours, beginning and ending at the Sloth Lounge. I carry a big black and white umbrella with the Sloth logo—a sloth with long eyelashes and large bosoms—to make me easy to follow.

So that's my new profession. So get out of the shower and come on down.

☉ Lagniappe ☉

If you happened to read one of my other two books, *Never Heave Your Bosom in a Front-Hook Bra*, or *Never Sleep with a Fat Man in July*, you might notice that the Fat Man of the title, which is my husband Lout, poor heart, hasn't shown up in this book yet.

There's a reason for that. It ain't a pretty story but, like they say, it is not for us mortals to know why stuff happens.

The last few chapters of this book—chapters I actually wrote before The Storm—will explain about Lout, and also about my gentleman friend, Lust.

How's that for some Lagniappe?

And like they say, God never opens a window without slamming the door first.

It was Good

Good trash is like fine wine. You can't just throw it out. You got to let it age awhile. Get good and ripe.

Everybody knows you can't just throw out a chicken wing and a half cup of rice with tomato gravy, right away, in cold blood. Anybody who does is wasteful and is the reason why there are people on the other side of the world going hungry.

You got to put them in a clean plastic container with a tight-fitting lid and burp that lid so no extra air don't get in and place it on the refrigerator shelf and leave it there until it grows green fuzz.

And then you can throw it out.

And stuff that isn't trash is even harder to get rid of. Like clothes that you are now too fat for—because naturally once you get rid of them you are going to have to stay fat.

And Mardi Gras beads.

And my husband Lout.

I got to explain. I have been putting off writing about this because it is so terrible. And the story ain't pretty, which Lout wasn't either, but I loved him anyway. The fact is, Lout has passed. Not as is passing a driver's test or gas or nothing. I mean he has passed away.

His mama, Ms. Larda, blames herself. And I blame myself. And Lout, wherever he is, is probably blaming himself. It was all our faults.

See, when her children was little, Ms. Larda didn't have a lot of money and she was a worrier, and she was afraid one of the kids would go out in the rain and catch their death, or she herself would plop over dead, and there wouldn't be no money to bury them. So she took out burial insurance on everybody.

Well, Lout kept up his insurance policy. He always said it was one thing he would definitely get to use some day. But then he got his mid-life crisis and all of a sudden he didn't want to think no more about things like that. I say to him one day, I say, I ain't seen no bills for burial insurance in a long time, did you let it lapse? Well, he don't want to admit I'm right, so he says he didn't. I say I bet he forgot about it and he says he did not, and may lightning strike him dead if he did.

He shouldn't have said that. Because he didn't and it did, right on the roof of the Sloth Lounge. It was during a Saints game. A thunderstorm come up and the screen blacked out just when they was actually about to score. And Lout is the one to rush up to the roof to fix the satellite dish. And ZAP!

So it turned out to be a good thing Lout didn't waste no more money on that burial insurance because he sort of got pre-cremated.

The Lord works in mysterious ways.

And terrible as it was, at least the funeral home gave us a big discount on putting Lout in a urn. But afterwards, we got the problem of where to keep him.

Now my mother-in-law Ms. Larda, she wants to put him on her mantlepiece, but her mantlepiece ain't wide enough. My Lout was a big man, and even powdered, he took up a lot of space.

His friends at the Sloth Lounge want the urn up on the back bar between the gin and the tequila, but Ms. Larda don't like that idea. So they retired his barstool instead.

And then I think about how Lout loved water, especially with Scotch. So we decided to scatter his ashes on the river.

On a gloomy Saturday afternoon, I never will forget, Ms. Larda and me and the rest of the family and a bunch of friends, all dressed in black, we get on the Mississippi River ferry, and line up by the rail. Ms. Larda is very worried because she heard dumping ashes in the river is illegal. I am standing there sobbing with the urn clutched to my bosom and Ms. Larda, she whispers real loud that we should all just try to look normal. I don't think we look too normal, but we don't get arrested.

And then I can't get the lid off the urn—they really ought to put shaker lids on them things, like on parmesan cheese. Ms. Larda snatches it away and she almost drops it and I think this urn is going to land in the water and Lout will float away like a genie in a bottle. But she gets the lid off, and the two of us dump Lout in and most of him sinks like a stone.

Then we all go home and we sit down around the kitchen table having a good cry in our ice-cold beers. The phone rings and it is this woman named Maybelline, a lady friend of Lout's that I never did care for. And she asks for Loutie.

I say as a matter of fact I just carried him over to the river and threw him in. And then I tell her good-bye.

I am too upset to mention he was dead and cremated first.

So if you hear any false rumors about me and Lout, they ain't true.

Good-bye, Lout. It was good.

No Longer Rerunning Scared

God is like a sitcom writer. When he runs out of new plots for your life, you go into reruns.

You get born, you grow up, you learn how to put on makeup and suck in your stomach and stick out your assets, and you start going out on dates.

I did it all once. And now I am in reruns. Because I am single again.

It took a long time to get around to it. After my late husband Lout, poor heart, got himself fried by that lightning bolt which he brung on himself, fooling with the satellite dish on top of the Sloth Lounge during a thunderstorm, I am so prostate with grief I am eating a entire box of Goo Goo Clusters a day for comfort.

My sister-in-law Gloriosa, she comes over and she explains how she can understand about my prostate problem but either I got to get on with life, or I will weigh as much as the combined population of Cicely, Alaska. There is a new manager named Ralf at the Sloth Lounge and he wants me to come over and be guest bartender on the anniversary of Lout's passing. I am going to decline, but Gloriosa says it is time to get out there and meet some grown-ups. What she means is men.

Then she prances into my bedroom and yanks open my underwear drawer and says for starters, all my underwear from Wal-Mart has finally sprung holes, and I got to go to Victoria's Secret in the New Orleans Centre for some fancy lingerie.

Well. Last time I was dating it was a mortal sin to so much as get kissed before the third date. At that rate, it will be a long time before anybody sees my underwear. But she says this is simply so I will feel attractive from the inside out, and it ain't got nothing to do with my moral behavior.

Then my teenage daughter Gumdrop chimes in and says it would be a good time to get my hair out of the age of dinosaurs. Now I have always gotten my hair done by Awlette at Hairy Problems, but no, that ain't good enough, she knows this salon which will do it right. It is at the New Orleans Centre too.

I always wondered about that place. How come they don't spell "center" right? Gloriosa says don't be ridiculous, "centre" is the European way. I guess nobody ever got hooked on phonics in Europe.

But we go to this beauty salon at the Centre anyway, and the lady there looks at me the way a emergency room nurse would look at a basket case.

See, I got hair that knows already exactly what it wants to do in life and that is flop in my eyes. Up to now Awlette pushed it back and made it stay put with so much hair spray that Hurricane Betsy couldn't move it. This lady, she decides to give me a natural look, which turns out to mean my hair flops in my eyes, but in a sexy way that Gloriosa and Gumdrop approve of.

Then we go to get my face redone at the makeup counter at Macy's. Now if my face was my fortune, I would have been sleeping under a bridge a long time ago. I ain't hoping for much—maybe midway between Mother Theresa and Tammy Faye Baker. But when she finishes, Gloriosa and Gumdrop say I am absolutely gorgeous.

Finally, we hit Victoria's Secret, where they ain't much into secrets as far as I can see. They let everything hang right out. The salesclerk say do I want a "teddy" and she ain't talking about no bear. "Your sweetie will like it," she says, and I say, "He can wear it then," and I am ready to go. But Gloriosa has already picked out bikini drawers and this wonderful bra which is supposed to lift and support and make the most of what I got. Which ain't much. I went to a entire prom once with my dress on backwards and nobody noticed the little pointy parts of my dress was sticking out over my shoulder blades until I got home.

But Gloriosa says once I put on this bra no man will ever look me in the eye again, because they will not be able to rip their attention away from my glorious bosom. I don't believe it, but then I put it on, and I am converted. I got a miracle on my chest. I look in the mirror, and the Modine looking back at me has got the potential for becoming a fallen woman.

I decide I better pray. Fast. I leave Gloriosa and Gumdrop shopping and I walk all the way to the Jesuit Church on Baronne Street, and I slip in a pew and kneel, but every time I bow my head I see this sexy bosom staring up at me. Finally I go up the side aisle to light a candle for the repose of Lout's soul. A nice-looking young priest comes out a confessional and passes me and I say, "Good afternoon, Father," and he says, "Good afternoon, bosom" and then he turns red as a beet and hurries off. I am thunderstruck. This is obviously a message from above.

That evening, I go to the Sloth. There is a man on the roof fooling with the satellite dish. But he don't get killed. Instead, he climbs down and walks up to me and smiles at my bosom and says, "Modine. A pleasure. My name is Lust. Ralf Lust."

The reruns are over.

Wedding Priorities

People always cry at weddings. Especially bridesmaids. They got reason to cry. They are standing in front of God and everybody in a dress that cost two months' salary, and it is specifically chosen to make them look terrible.

Now, I know how brides think, because I was once one myself. This is YOUR day. And you, come hell or high water, are going to be the prettiest girl in the room.

This means one of two things. Either you choose real ugly bridesmaids, so even if your wedding day turns out to be the mother of all bad hair days and you have broke out in zits, you are still going to look good by comparison. Or you choose your true friends, even if they are pretty, and then you do your best to ugly them up. This is why bridesmaids' dresses are usually some color like slime green, and designed to emphasize the stomach, flatten the bosom, and broaden the shoulders so everybody looks as feminine as Arnold Schwarzenegger in ruffles.

Even so, my sister-in-law Gloriosa don't get asked to be in many weddings. Gloriosa is so drop-dead gorgeous that no matter how she's dressed, once she jiggles up the aisle, nobody will take their eyes off her. Not even if the bride marches in stark naked and playing a trumpet.

But my other sister-in-law Larva, who looks like Rosie O'Donnell, gets asked to be in more weddings than she can shake a stick at. Which she don't appreciate too much, even though she is too nice to say no, because, besides having to pay for the awful dress, she got to ante up for a couple of showers and a bachelorette party. She says they ought to let bridesmaids get in on the money dance. They are the ones who need the money.

But when Cousin Lotta took the leap, both Gloriosa and Larva had to be in the wedding. For one thing, it was a very important Uptown wedding at Our Lady of Prompt Succor Chapel. Besides being cousins, both Gloriosa and Larva happen to be old friends with the groom, Ralph Duke.

The Dukes are Uptown people, so everything has to be perfect, Mrs. Duke says. No beer. No money dance. No throwing rice, because birds eat it and it isn't good for them. Instead, a flock of snow white doves will be released when the happy couple dashes outside.

And besides bridesmaids, there will be tastefully dressed lectors to read Bible verses. Tasteful turns out to mean black graduation gowns hanging below the knees. Naturally, Gloriosa gets asked to be a lector. And Larva gets to be a bridesmaid.

My mother-in-law Ms. Larda is standing in for the mother of the bride since Lotta's real mother run off with her Orkin man years ago. And Ms. Larda says she don't understand this Uptown stuff, but she is going to be as helpful as she can. So she volunteers to arrange for 12 white doves.

She orders them from DeeDee's Flowers, Balloons and Special Effects for Special Occasions. The day of the wedding she calls DeeDee again, to make sure them doves will be there as soon as the new Mr. and Mrs. Duke get down the aisle.

But Ms. Larda is the victim of three unfortunate coincidences. The first is she always pronounces "aisle" like it was "erl." The second is that this singer called the Duke of Earl—remember him?—is in town. The third is that DeeDee has already got two orders to send the Duke of Earl stuff at his hotel. And DeeDee's clerk is so star-struck, when she hears the words "duke" and "erl" in the same sentence, she thinks it is another order for him, and sends the doves to his hotel.

Well, the wedding is about as beautiful as it can be with six bridesmaids skulking around in slime green. When Gloriosa struts to the altar, she is wearing a low-cut red dress under her graduation gown. Nobody would have known this if she had buttoned up the front of the gown like she was supposed to. But instead, she lets it hang off her shoulders like a cape, and she causes a stir which Lotta never knows about because by that part of the ceremony, she is up front with her back to everybody.

Meanwhile, Ms. Larda realizes the doves ain't coming, so she sends my brothers-in-law Leech and Lurch over to Audubon Park with a lot of bird seed and a cat carrier. Just in time, they come back with six pigeons.

I don't know what kind of bird seed they use, but it must affect them pigeons like a laxative. Or else the cat smell in the carrier made them very nervous. Anyway, when they swarm out over the heads of the wedding party, everybody starts shrieking and running for cover. The bride and groom have to make a running leap into the limo. I myself think they would rather have been pelted with rice.

Later, Larva says she is just as glad it happened because now she don't never have to wear that dress again.

Maybe they got reasons for the way they do things Uptown.

A Vision at Celibacy Academy

When the Blessed Mother turned up missing from home economics class, Sister Scrupula decided enough was enough.

This wasn't your everyday kind of Blessed Mother. This one was made completely of Rice Krispies—except for her glow-in-the-dark rosary—by Celibacy Academy's senior class of 1965. She was 18 inches tall, and perfect in every detail.

Sister Scrupula, the home ec teacher, decided it would be disrespectful to serve her at the graduation reception, so she sprayed her with bug repellent and put her in a place of honor on top of the tall cabinet in the home ec lab, where she would inspire future students like myself. I was a junior in 1965.

The Blessed Mother vanished the very next day.

Sister's office was right next to the home ec lab, and she had noticed things missing before—a couple cups of pecans and some cooking sherry and such, but never a entire Blessed Mother. She decided she was dealing with a crime wave, so she took emergency money out of her home ec budget, and she ordered one of them trick mirrors that shows your reflection from one side, while somebody you can't see is staring at you from the other side.

She arranged to have it installed between her office and the lab, so she could wait and watch when people went in to work on projects by themselves.

Then Sister unexpectedly got transferred, and by the time the mirror arrived that summer, she was on her way to a missionary school in the Fiji Islands.

The maintenance workers installed it anyway. But without her to glare over their shoulders, they made a mistake. They put it in backward.

This means everybody in the home ec lab could look into her office, but the person in her office just saw a mirror. That was the year Celibacy Academy—which is a all-girls' school—got its first male teacher, Coach Glubber. And he got assigned to Sister's old office.

For the first couple weeks of school, a lot of people did extra work in home ec. Before this, the closest thing to manhood we had seen on campus was a few of the older nuns who had sprouted mustaches.

Anyway, it turned out watching the coach was as

exciting as looking at our own fathers sitting in front of the Friday night fights. He was kind of pudgy and at least 40. After awhile, we just forgot about him. Every now and then one of us glanced up and was startled by his face a few inches away checking for stubble on his chin, but most of the stuff he did was pretty dull.

Until November. Which is when he recruited some young men from Holy Repression Prep to help coach our basketball team. This team, like all the Celibacy Academy teams, had almost no players because our all-purpose athletic uniform was so modest it was embarrassing. It was a one-piece outfit that included culottes to disguise the fact we actually had crotches, and also to cover us if, in the course of playing the game, we found it necessary to raise one of our legs.

But once we got real boys in the gym, three-fourths of the school wanted to play basketball. Anyway, Coach Glubber was smarter than he looked.

But not smart enough. When the boys came over in their khaki uniforms, he sent them into his office to change into their shorts and t-shirts.

I was in the lab after school the first day they came. I had been sick and missed the pecan pie class so I had to bake a makeup pie.

I looked up and—lo and behold—instead of Coach Glubber, I see five high school boys, stripping down and glimpsing at the mirror to check themselves over. I was checking them over too. I knew it was a sin, but I couldn't stop.

Afterwards, there was no way I could keep it to myself, so I decided to tell just one person. Unfortunately, I picked my friend Awlette, who I now refer to as the Mouth of the South.

The next day we got 40 people in the home ec lab after school. And one of them was Tammy Zeefle, editor of the yearbook, who decided to take a picture. With a flashbulb. Well, the one thing you are not supposed to do when you are looking through a one-way mirror is flash a light, because it illuminates you. For a split second, these boys had a clear vision of 40 high school girls panting on the other side of the glass. I think it scared them.

Anyway, they must have ratted us out. Because the next day, Miss Pruitt announced we were ending the cooking half of the class immediately and were going to proceed with our sewing studies. Our first project was to make curtains for the window. So we got to clean the foodstuffs out of all the cabinets and replace them with sewing supplies. When we got to the front cabinet, Awlette climbed on top to be thorough and she let out a yell. She reached behind it, into a niche between the cabinet and the wall, and pulled out a glow-in-the-dark rosary. Under it was a pile of blue Rice Krispies. Somebody must have turned on the ceiling fan and the Blessed Mother blew over and fell in there. Rice Krispie Blessed Mothers don't weigh much.

Awlette said that explained why we got caught. The Blessed Mother was there all along—even if it was in the form of Rice Krispies—and she obviously don't approve of that kind of stuff.

I myself don't believe the Blessed Mother lurks in Rice Krispies. But we swept them all up and put them in a box and mailed them to the Fiji Islands.

No sense taking chances.

Marriage? Don't Ask

One good thing about being a single woman with a gentleman friend is this: if he don't got clean drawers, it's not your fault.

When my husband, Lout, God rest his soul, was alive, and he opened his bureau and discovered no clean drawers, it was definitely my fault. I would rush to the dirty clothes pile next to my washing machine, pull out a pair of drawers, sprinkle a few drops of bleach on it, wave it over my head a few times, and hand it to him, smelling all nice and fresh.

I don't have to do shameful things like that no more. Everybody is responsible for their own drawers. That is one very good argument for not getting married.

My gentleman friend, Lust, happened to be at my house last year, on the morning of New Year's Eve while I was putting away the Christmas stuff. (It would be the last time I would put away this Christmas stuff, but we didn't know that yet.) I was showing him this cute little ornament that was a mouse in a Christmas hat.

Just then, a real live mouse scuttled across my floor. Well. I stepped calmly up on the coffee table and asked Lust to take care of it, please, in a kind of loud screechy voice. Naturally, Lust had to ask if I didn't think this mouse was "cute." By the time he stopped laughing, the mouse had gone to God knows where.

Very funny.

My daughter Gumdrop had just moved back to New Orleans with her husband Slime, and they were staying with me until their place would be ready. Gumdrop was about to have my first grandchild, and I don't want her waddling around and stepping on no mouse.

So after Lust goes off to the Sloth Lounge, the bar which he owns, to get ready for that night, I make a mistake. I ask my brother-in-law Leech to get rid of this mouse.

Now Leech ain't usually successful with anything he tries, but this time he pulls back the couch, sees the mouse, slams a coffee mug over it, and has it captured. He is about to call me into the room and tell me. Then he stops. He's got one of his ideas. He has read somewheres that a baby born on New Year's Day gets a lot of prizes. Gumdrop is going to have this baby any time and this mouse might just get her started. Shock therapy. He slides a magazine under the cup, flips it over, goes across the street to his house and dumps the mouse into a little box along with some Velveeta cheese and a grape, and takes it home.

Next day, the whole family gets together at my place to watch the football games on my new TV. I put out some of my mother-in-law's black-eyed peas and cabbage and some pork rinds on the sideboard for us all to eat.

Then, wouldn't you know, the TV picture goes haywire. Lust gets down on the floor to fool with the row of buttons under the screen. I bring him the directions that came with the set and he spreads them out on the floor between his legs while he punches buttons. The rest of us help ourselves to the food.

And Leech decides this is the time to give Gumdrop her jump-start. He sets the mouse loose on the floor near where she is standing. And it runs right over her foot. But she got shoes on, and she can't see her feet, and she don't even notice it.

None of us do.

Then it runs up Lust's right pants leg.

He notices it.

Now, I got to tell you something private about Lust. He don't wear jockey drawers. He thinks they are too confining. He wears boxers. And if he don't have no clean ones, being as he don't have a wife in charge of his underwear, he sometimes goes commando, like they say. So I don't know if he had on any actual drawers or not, but I got my suspicions.

Anyway, Lust grabs at his crotch. At the same time, he levitates into the air with his legs still apart, which I would not have believed if I had not seen it, and then he stomps real fast like them Irish river dancers. All this time he is yelling. I haven't heard yelling like that since my mother-in-law mistook the TV remote for one of the kids' video games and started pushing buttons just when the Saints were kicking for the winning point.

Leech, meanwhile, has chosen to leave the house without explaining. And the rest of us, who still don't realize there is a mouse involved, assume Lust has gone out of his mind.

The mouse exits out his left pants leg, but with all the carrying on, none of us see it. Lust grabs up my broom and starts chasing this mouse, which is running in circles.

Now Lust is a big man, so when he commences tearing around and slamming the broom against the floor, we all decide to beat it out of there. We are as far as the outside steps when the noise stops.

I peek back around the doorsill, and Lust is flopped backward across the couch breathing heavy, and the broom is lying on the floor, broken in two places. While I am looking, I see the mouse hustle past me and disappear into my azalea bed.

A light bulb turns on over my head, and I understand.

So I go inside, and I get a cold beer out the fridge. I sit beside Lust and pass it over. And I don't say a word. Here is what I don't say:

"Do YOU think the mouse is 'cute'?"

"Maybe you should wear jockey drawers."

And he don't say, "Will you marry me and wash my drawers?"

We understand each other.

About the Author

Modine Gunch was created by Liz Scott Monaghan as a way to tell stories that she otherwise wouldn't repeat in company, mixed or otherwise. She has kept readers of *New Orleans Magazine* chuckling for nearly 25 years.

Before Hurricane Katrina hit, Modine led a sitcom sort of life in Chalmette, a New Orleans suburb. Afterward, she bobbed up in a different part of town, wetter and wiser but sassy as ever. And so did Liz, who lives nearby on the closest thing she can find to a hill.

For more about Modine Gunch, go to
www.modineg.com.